PLANTING DESIGN

PLANTING DESIGN

Brian Hackett

Emeritus Professor of Landscape Architecture,
University of Newcastle-upon-Tyne

New York

McGRAW-HILL BOOK COMPANY

First published in the United States of America 1979
by McGraw-Hill Book Company
1221 Avenue of the Americas, New York, N.Y. 10020

Printed in Great Britain

Library of Congress Cataloging in Publication Data

Hackett, Brian.
   Planting design.

Includes bibliographical references and index.
   1. Landscape gardening. 2. Landscape architecture.
   3. Plants, Ornamental. I. Title.
   SB472.H17 1979   715   78-26625
   ISBN 0-07-025402-8

Contents

Preface

The bookshops are flooded each year with excellent books on trees, shrubs and other types of plants used in gardens and larger landscapes; these explain the methods of planting and after care, and describe the appearance of the plants. But few attempts have been made to explain how different plants can be selected and planted in landscapes as a contribution to an appearance which meets the aesthetic principles of the designer while entering into favourable relationships with the habitat and with the other plants.

Planting design cannot be separated from landscape design and planning in practice, but its many facets, such as analysing the appearance of individual plants and exploring how plants may or may not be good neighbours, can be studied in depth. With this background, the designer can support his intuitive decisions on planting with a basis of principles.

My work over some 30 years with students of landscape design brought me face to face with the task of explaining from the ecological and appearance points of view why some plants are good neighbours in a landscape and others are not. The lively mind of the student is not satisfied with rambling discussions on this or that in planting design – he expects to be given a reason for everything, or at least to be told why one is unable to give a reason. Nor is the student taken in by an overdose of superb pictures of planting when he needs to know why they are so superb. Thus, I have now found the opportunity to set down the results of teaching the subject in Britain and the U.S.A. for so many years, supported by a long period of applying theory to practice.

As I have said, planting design has many facets, and these cannot all be discussed at one and the same time. Thus, questions of the colour and texture of plants are discussed in this book somewhat in isolation before relating these aspects of a plant to other plants in a sympathetic manner.

The principles of planting design are, in general, applicable to all parts of the world, although the habitat conditions, such as the soil and climate, determine what plants will grow in a particular place. In giving examples of plants to illustrate a particular point, I have necessarily drawn on plants with which I am familiar in the British Isles, but it will not be difficult for readers in other countries to identify their own examples. In order to simplify the task of reading, plants are referred to in the text by their common name where one exists, with the botanical nomenclature added for the first time a plant is mentioned. The knowledge and experience needed for planting methods and techniques in a variety of situations is extensive, and is well covered in the literature. Thus, I have only referred to the practical and technical matters when the design has a particular relevance to them beyond the normal growth and after care operations.

I would like to think that this book keeps alive the pioneer work of Professor Florence B. Robinson in seeking principles upon which planting design can be based. Her two books on the subject, 'Planting Design' and 'Palette of Plants', have long been out of print in their modestly produced Mid-West editions since she gave them to me in 1949. She would have been the first to say that the considerable growth all over the world in the number of persons involved in planting decisions in landscape has added to the knowledge that she gathered together so many years ago.

CHAPTER 1

Planting design through the ages

The selection and arrangement of trees, shrubs and other plants in a landscape can be considered as the detailing of the landscape design, although a design philosophy which considers the layout of the landscape together with the plants, hard surfaces and artefacts as one exercise is regarded today as the right way to proceed. It is difficult to separate planting design from landscape design, but there are examples in the past, and indeed today, in which it is clear that the plants were to grow in a manner unlike their natural habitat after the landscape design had been finalized, and thus were selected as a later and separate exercise. The layout of these landscape designs may have survived, but the planting will have changed many times through age and fashion, and because the provision for planting did not favour the regeneration of the plants. Thus, our knowledge of the planting of landscapes laid out more than two or three hundred years ago is limited, and is derived from such varied sources as the written word, old paintings, and the continuation of tradition in remote places. The reconstructed gardens of Colonial Williamsburg, Virginia, in the U.S.A. are examples of careful historical research.

1.1. Formal planting

The evidence about planting that is available from ancient times suggests that plants were used to define and highlight formal patterns, particularly by the repetition of one species at equal intervals (Fig. 1.1). In the days of Ancient Rome, the art of topiary carried this approach to planting to the stage where landscape design became a form of building design. The Romans did, however, record an interest in plants which produce easily-visible flowers, and if no design principles governed the selection of the species, the plants were contained within the framework of a formal landscape design.

When the Dark Ages gave way to the cultural revival of the Age of Humanism in Europe, there is evidence that the new liberalism was reflected in a less contrived approach to planting. In Italy, during the 15th century, there is evidence of an interest in wild flowers being allowed and encouraged

1

Fig. 1.1 Through the ages plants have often been arranged so that the same species occur at equal intervals, as in this example.

to grow in grassed areas, and of evergreen Holm oak (*Quercus ilex*) woodlands being accepted as part of a 'designed' landscape. Soon, however, the planting changed with the selection of a single species to be used for filling a space in a pattern. The species used were often selected for their ability to maintain the pattern, and included evergreen plants and those which would grow with a close texture after clipping. In the 17th century, the pattern, or parterre as it is better known (Fig. 1.2), was more often defined by box (*Buxus sempervirens*) edging. While in France the parterre dominated large areas of the landscape, in Italy it was usually surrounded by woodland (Fig. 1.3) with an informal silhouette created by cypresses (*Cupressus* spp.) and pines (*Pinus* spp.).

Some other developments in planting that are associated with Italian gardens of the Renaissance were the use of fruit trees for visual effect as well as to produce fruit, and plants in pots and tubs were used in gardens as though they were works of sculpture. The cypress avenue was another form of planting and directed attention to a view beyond the garden or to some feature in the garden, and to a certain extent reduced the strong visual effect of planting arranged to form a pattern.

1.2. The individual plant

The evidence from the garden landscapes of the Far East discloses an interest in planting design in the visual effect of one plant in relation to another plant (Fig. 1.4), compared with the emphasis on arranging plants to

Fig. 1.2 An example of 'parterre' planting, in which the pattern is defined by the low shrub edging (courtesy of the National Trust).

Fig. 1.3 Formal parterre areas in the gardens of Italy during the Renaissance were usually surrounded with woodland planting, similar to this tree belt around an English lawn.

3

Fig. 1.4 A Japanese garden which illustrates the care in the selection and placing of plants in landscape associated with the Far East.

accord with a pattern, which happened in the European civilizations. The preponderance of conifers and broad-leaved evergreens in the gardens of the Far East demonstrated a concern for the Winter effect, and also for the subtlety of the textural effects of the leaves and for the gentle modulation of green colours towards yellow and blue. But the major consideration seems to have been the contrasts between the form of the various plants and the habit or line effects brought out so well in the brushwork of the artists, for example, a twisted and rugged pine tree which had been planted near to a spreading cherry (*Prunus* spp.) or a weeping willow (e.g. *Salix matsudana 'Pendula'*). Much the same principles were applied to the smaller plants, such as the water lily (*Nuphar japonicum*), the veronica (*Hebe murorum*), *Pteris aquilinia*, and bamboos (e.g. *Arundinaria angustifolia*), decorative grasses and mosses.

Short-lived seasonal effects of strong visual contrast (Plate 1) were more sought after in the gardens of the Far East compared with the slower and more gentle changes of the later herbaceous borders and rose gardens of the West. Trees like the lilacs (*Syringa* spp.), laburnum (*Laburnum* spp.), almond (*Prunus dulcis*) and peach (e.g. *Prunus persica*) were planted for Spring effect, and maples (*Acer palmatum* and *rufinerve*) for Autumn effect. The Spring effect was further emphasised by groundflora, such as the wild hyacinth (*Scilla* spp.), violets (*Viola* spp.) and primroses (*Primula* spp.).

The association between the landscape designs of the Far East and the natural landscape is familiar to those interested in the history of landscapes,

4

especially in the stylized simulation of mountain and river landscapes, and also the philosophy embodied in this association. On a smaller scale, this philosophy influenced the planting design. The plant we call Jew's mallow (*Kerria japonica*) and *Lespedeza formosa* when planted near to a stream were meant to convey the idea of a river landscape, and mounds planted with cherries and maples signified a mountain landscape. Clipped evergreen shrubs were planted among rocks to represent islands and hills. There was also an association between certain plants and a particular situation, like *Rhododendron indicum* and the fern (*Polypodium lingua*) at the base of stones.

1.3. Planting in Moslem gardens

Plants were also used for symbolic purposes in the Moslem gardens of the Middle East and India; considerable ingenuity must have been used because the landscape design was formal and uncomplicated, compared with the informal subtleties of the Far East. Yet an association between different plant species and their groupings with mystical ideas was present, and the way in which plants were allowed to develop naturally within the formal pattern gave a visual expression to a variety of mystical ideas. The hot climate was also a vital influence in the planting, necessitating a close connection between the plants and the irrigation channels.

A matter of considerable interest in the planting of the gardens of the Middle East and India was the effect of bright light in the day, and the contrast brought about by the darkness at night. In order to achieve the desired visual interest in the day, plants with strong coloured flowers were used, and for night and dusk effects, many white flowered species were added.

The cultural links between the Middle East and Spain were evident in the Moorish civilization which dominated many parts of the country from the 8th to the 13th centuries A.D. Nevertheless, there were significant differences in the use of plants. One influence may have been the fact that most of the gardens in the Middle East and India were laid out on level ground, whereas in Spain the Moors not only found a hilly terrain but also the requirements of defence, and preserving their identity in a foreign country, were some of the likely reasons for small gardens in enclosed spaces. A natural consequence of the latter situation would be a refined and close interest in a few plants and their arrangement in order to achieve maximum visual interest (Fig. 1.5).

The native vegetation of southern Spain was not very rich in the number of different species suitable for gardens compared with the more temperate and fertile areas. Exotic plants were brought from as far away as Syria and India in order that a more comprehensive selection was available – handled with a skill equal to that evident in the decorated tiles and richly patterned rugs and carpets used to such telling effect in the shade of the rooms and colonnades. Similarly, the illumination contrasts referred to previously

5

Fig. 1.5 A Spanish courtyard garden, in which there is interest in selecting and arranging a few plants in a sensitive manner.

between night and day, were taken into account in the strong contrasts between light and shade in the garden areas. It is not possible to be certain about the details of the planting so many years ago, but the happy relationships achieved in the contemporary reconstructions keep alive the tradition. The planting now includes such diverse plant forms as clipped evergreen hedges, deciduous shrubs like roses (*Rosa* spp.) allowed to grow naturally, and plants in moveable flower pots. The use of the latter is well suited to the short flowering period of many of the exotics, and these are often spectacular in appearance and contrast with the shrubs and hedges. Tree planting was arranged to provide maximum shade, as would be expected.

1.4. The green landscape

In these historical examples from the Far East and the Moslem world, the interest was in the individual plants as well as in their ability to contribute to the realization of the landscape design, except where grouped effect and function were paramount, with topiary and tree planting primarily for shade. With the emergence of the English School of Landscape of the 18th century, plants – in the sense of individuals – were replaced by a very limited range of tree species in groups and belts. Grassed parks with deciduous trees, whose potential monotony was avoided by topographical variety and lakes and streams, were the main elements of the landscape design. This description does not do justice to some innovations in planting which were introduced from time to time. The Cedar of Lebanon (*Cedrus libani*) and the evergreen Holm oak are two grand specimen trees that were known in Britain in the middle of the 17th century; towards the end of his life, the 6th Earl of Haddington (died 1735) expressed an interest in flowering trees and shrubs, and in the yellow stemmed willows (*Salix alba 'Vitellina'*); the Hon. Charles Hamilton at Painshill in Surrey in the middle of the 18th century planted trees and shrubs that were new to Britain (Fig. 1.6) – in contrast to Capability Brown's familiar manner of planting as many as 100 000 trees on one estate, using mostly one or two species, such as beech (*Fagus sylvatica*), oak (*Quercus* spp.) or pine. Henry Hoare at another famous example of the English School of Landscape – Stourhead in Wiltshire – also moved a step away from the bare trees and grass to add cherry laurel (*Prunus laurocerasus*) underplanting.

While the practitioners of the English School of Landscape were using a limited range of plant species, a few botanical gardens and, of course, the traditional cottage garden (Fig. 1.7) contained a wider range. Certainly by the end of the first quarter of the 18th century, the importation of exotics into Britain from abroad had commenced, especially from North America. In 1765 the collection at Whitton, near Hounslow, listed 342 different plant species, and by 1768 the Royal garden at Kew had over 3000 different species with the precise figure of 5535 in 1789. More interesting to planting design, however, was the record of Dr. John Fothergill's garden laid out in 1762 at Upton House, East Ham, because this included a wild area in which

Fig. 1.6 The effect created by the introduction of exotic tree species into Britain from the latter part of the 18th century.

Fig. 1.7 Planting associated with the traditional cottage garden.

hardy exotics successfully naturalized. Dr. Fothergill also cultivated alpine plants.

The landowners of the 18th century in the rural areas were not alone in the contribution they made to increasing the range of plant species available for planting landscape designs, because the employers, and their employees, of the new manufacturing industries were also active in an interest in plants. In particular, expensive plants like unusual tulip bulbs were associated with the employers, and the hybridization of varieties of auricula (*Primula auricula* var.), carnations (*Dianthus caryophyllus* var.), pinks (*Dianthus plumarius* var.) and polyanthus (*Primula vulgaris elatior* var.) with their employees.

1.5. Introduction of exotics

The end of the 18th century and the early years of the 19th century in Britain were significant for a change in the traditional planting of deciduous tree species (Fig. 1.8). The Winter appearance of landscapes was to be changed when trees like the conifers, the red silver fir (*Abies amabilis*), Monterey pine (*Pinus radiata*), Sitka spruce (*Picea sitchensis*), Western red cedar (*Thuja plicata*), and Lawson's cypress (*Chamaecyparis lawsoniana*) grew up, and these were introduced from abroad and planted at this time. This new development occurred at the same time as the formal garden began to reappear around large houses, and which provided the opportunity to introduce a wide range of the smaller plants. At the same time, industry was developing rapidly, and the inventions and new ideas in various design fields that accompanied this development were matched in gardens by

Fig. 1.8 Trees such as the western hemlock (*Tsuga heterophylla*) when introduced into Britain significantly changed the traditional deciduous landscape.

experimentation with more and more exotic plants – to the extent that experimentation frequently overrode sensitivity in the selection of plant species and in the way they were associated together. It was a time when man delighted in exercising over Nature his newly found power; he was unmindful of the fact that his garden and larger landscape projects were not entirely new works, but were just another modification of a long established landscape which changed, sometimes slowly and sometimes quickly, in response to climate and man's social changes.

1.6. Natural planting

During this period when the range of plants used in gardens increased, the interest of some people was concentrated on a particular family of plants such as *Rosa* species (the catalogue of Rivers and Son of Sawbridgeworth, Hertfordshire, in 1836 lists many species and varieties), and books by James Shirley Hibberd published later in the 19th century included the titles *The Fern Garden* (1869) and *The Ivy* (1872). But this concentration of interest, compared with several plant species grouped in a happy association based upon Nature's patterns or a visual effect, was countered during the latter part of the century as a result of the influence of William Robinson, Gertrude Jekyll and Reginald Farrer, with whom we associate planting expressed in 'the wild woodland garden' (Fig. 1.9), 'the herbaceous border', and 'the alpine garden'. These particular examples of planting design were

Fig. 1.9 This woodland garden illustrates the new developments in planting design introduced by William Robinson, Gertrude Jekyll and Reginald Farrer in the latter part of the 19th century.

far removed from the influence of geometry and building architecture, and allowed the planting to speak for itself.

Across the Atlantic Jens Jensen, working in the Chicago area of the U.S.A. from 1886, soon began to use native plants in his landscape projects. But particularly from 1905 his design approach embraced the natural prairie landscape of the Mid-West as the model, although he does not seem to have used prairie grasses. Nevertheless, he wrote late in life:

Leave the native growth alone, and fill in with oaks, sugar maple, cherry, ironwood, shad, hawthorne, plum and crab apple. Elm and ash for the low places. You may also use tulip, pepperidge, dogwood, and sassafras. Sycamore in low places. Hickories are difficult to plant, but they are a good mixture[1].

Jensen was not alone in the use of native plants in the U.S.A. for W. Miller, O. C. Simonds, and F. L. Olmsted must also be given credit for this important approach to planting design which has come to the fore again with an ecological emphasis from the middle of the present century.

A very different use of native plants was evident in the early work of Burle Marx, the Brazilian landscape architect, around 1937, when he collected wild plants which would form controlled abstract patterns on the surface of the ground instead of arranging the plants in mixed associations not too dissimilar from associations in natural landscapes. But in the contemporary scene, the less formal and contrived ideas of Robinson, Jensen and the others are relevant to the counter movement away from all that mechanization has brought, and to the economic and social change which has made the gardening operations for maintaining formalized planting so expensive, for example, as described in an account of the restoration of the formal gardens at Herrenhausen in Hanover, West Germany [2]. Thus, the use of wild plants, groundcover plants in place of neatly weeded earth, and the mass planting of a single species of shrub are typical of planting design today. There is also a more detailed concern for the visual interest of the individual plant and in the way it associates with another plant in both an ecological and visual sense.

References
[1] Christy, Stephen F. (1976), *Landscape Architecture U.S.A.*, January, 60–66.
[2] Gollwitzer, Gerda (1976) *Landscape Architecture U.S.A.,* May, 231–238.

CHAPTER 2
Natural plant relationships

Plants find their places in natural landscapes as a result of a number of factors such as the kind of soil, the orientation and amount of light, and the water table/drainage status; the places are then likely to be varied by the influence of birds, animals, insects and, indeed, by other plants. Ecology is the term used for these various events and reactions taking place in the landscape. As an essential aid to planting design, these factors and variables must be understood, together with an appraisal of the visual effects they create. There is always the tendency to value the whole appearance of a natural landscape without considering the ecological and visual interest at the scale of one plant in relation to another. Not only is there a wealth of visual variables among plants in natural landscapes, but the ways in which plants relate visually to one another in them leave little room for criticism.

2.1. Natural simplicity

The first observation that can be made is that the appearance of a group of different plants growing closely together in natural landscape has a unified quality without any distinct 'strangers' in colour or texture. There may be contrast, and numerous species, among the herbs of a prairie landscape, but as this generally occurs over a considerable area, the appearance also has the quality of simplicity. When a landscape has achieved the full climax state of high forest, the dominant trees may be few in number and limited to one species compared with the shrubs and groundcover layers, and they are visually as well as ecologically dominant; thus, the qualities of unity and simplicity again relate to this different kind of natural landscape.

If we compare typical examples of oak and beech-dominated natural woodlands, the former has, at densities of less than about 135 trees to the hectare, a rich and profuse shrub and herb layer due to the gentle shade cast by the mature oaks (Fig. 2.1), but at densities of more than this the canopy is thicker and the shrub layer is sparse, although the herb layer is well developed. Beech woodlands, on the other hand, show the opposite situation, with heavy shade except in the Winter and early Spring (Fig. 2.2); there is also very little shrub layer or groundcover, particularly on calcareous

Fig. 2.1 An old oak woodland in a natural state.

Fig 2.2 A beech woodland in early Spring, showing the limited groundflora and the shade-happy evergreen plants.

soils, except for the early Spring herbs, and where holly (*Ilex aquifolium*) and yew (*Taxus baccata*) are present as shade-happy plants, making a strong contrast in Winter. Sometimes the soil determines the relationship between the different types of vegetation – pine trees growing well on a sandy soil, but little else. An interesting exception is the grass groundcover below the Douglas fir belt in the Rocky Mountains of the U.S.A. (Fig. 2.3), where the pine (*Pinus ponderosa*) climax has widely spaced trees and thus allows light to penetrate.

Distinct height differences between the dominant and sub-dominant tree layers, the shrub layer, and the groundcover or herb layer simplify the appearance of a woodland. An alder (*Alnus glutinosa*) woodland, however, does not have such a clear hierarchical division; shrubs like sallow (*Salix caprea*), alder buckthorn (*Rhamnus frangula*), and the guelder rose (*Viburnum opulus*) occupy nearly as important a place, with a rich herb layer of nettles (*Urtica dioica*), meadowsweet (*Filipendula ulmaria*) and flags (*Iris pseudacorus*). The fact that the alder, like hazel (*Corylus avellana*), sometimes grows with multiple stems thus gives to this type of woodland a substantial vertical character, joining together in a visual sense the rest of the plants.

The qualities of simplicity and unity among plants in natural landscapes are most easily seen when the habitat conditions are unfriendly or at the acid or alkaline extremes of the average soils. Familiar examples are gorse (*Ulex europaeus*) or broom (*Cytisus scoparius*) scrub dominating an infertile slope

Fig. 2.3 Pine forest in the Rocky Mountains of the U.S.A. with a grass groundcover.

of exposed subsoil, or upland conditions of acid soils favouring ericaceous species. These qualities are also seen in the similarity in size of the plants in thickets; for example, blackthorn (*Prunus spinosa*), hawthorn (*Crataegus monogyna*), gorse, bramble (*Rubus fruticosus*) and wild roses, and this kind of mass effect, at not too great a height, is significant for the scale of planting required for many contemporary landscape designs. Blackthorn deserves further mention as a plant which emerges from a thicket or woodland because of its suckering inclinations – in visual terms this brings about a sensitive change from tall woodland to the herb layer of an adjacent open landscape.

The Californian redwood (*Sequoia sempervirens*) is another example of a natural landscape with qualities of simplicity and unity. The red/brown colour of the tall trunks relates admirably to the dark green of the trees, shrubs and groundcover plants, such as the tanbark oak (*Lithocarpus densiflorus*), the rhododendron (*Rhododendron californicum*), the gaultheria (*Gaultheria shallon*), the blueberry (*Vaccinium angustifolium*) and the fern (*Polystichum munitum*).

2.2. The dominant in planting

Many of the dominant trees in natural landscapes succeed in maintaining their status over a range of altitude and soil type differences, and in these landscapes the dominant is the medium which provides the qualities of simplicity and unity when the other species change. Oakwoods, for example, include the stunted oaks and rich herb layer of grass and ferns of Wistman's

Wood on a Dartmoor valley side in Devonshire, and also the high altitude oakwoods with an ericaceous groundcover. Other examples with the oak as the dominant tree are the damp oakwoods in the mild climate of south-west Eire with holly and the strawberry tree (*Arbutus unedo*) as a secondary layer[1].

2.3. Contrast in nature

Contrast is a visual effect often sought by designers, and there are many examples worthy of study in natural landscapes. A beech woodland in early Spring has a conspicuous groundcover such as wood anemone (*Anemone nemorosa*) or the introduced snowdrop (*Galanthus nivalis*) which contrast with the tall and bare tree trunks; even when a beech woodland has an understorey of English yew or holly, there is the evergreen contrast in Winter. A different kind of contrast, sometimes occurring on light acid soils, is bracken (*Pteridium aquilinum*) growing through a tangle of brambles which might suggest a fern groundlayer under the trees with shrubs well spaced as an interesting possibility in planting design. Contrast is also seen in landscapes which are in a stage of reversion from human disturbance to their natural state, and exemplified by the junipers (*Juniperus communis*) with their vertical habit on the Lüneberg Heath in West Germany (Fig. 2.4), contrasting with the heather (*Erica* spp.) groundcover – a landscape at risk from the invasion of birch (*Betula pendula*) with its contrast of pale leaves and bark. The invasion of gorse or hawthorn into neglected grassland is a

Fig. 2.4 The contrast between the junipers and the grass groundcover is a feature of the Lüneberg Heath in West Germany.

familiar visual contrast and, once established, the spiny character of these plants enables them to resist normal grazing.

The design of a planting plan so that contrasts are achieved by a succession of different seasonal effects is a familiar and acceptable policy – many examples occur in natural landscapes. Gorse, which has already been mentioned, provides another effect of contrast with its blanket of yellow flowers in the Spring, although there is little contrast in the vegetational pattern over the rest of the year. An ashwood (*Fraxinus excelsior*), on the other hand, has a succession of frequent but gentle contrasts because the trees, coming late into leaf and with light foliage, allow the growth of rich and varied herb and shrub layers. The ash can accept drainage conditions varying from marsh to dry soils with corresponding contrasts in the groundflora. Another example of contrast in the groundflora occurs in birchwoods, varying from grasses, bluebells (*Scilla nonscripta*), bilberry or cowberry (*Vaccinium vitis idaea*) to bracken.

2.4. Seasonal interest

Seasonal contrast and interest in natural landscapes can present a very comprehensive picture throughout the year (Plate 2). In a typical beech (*Fagus grandifolia*) and sugar maple (*Acer sacchorum*) forest in North America, the shrub layers able to succeed in the heavy Summer shade from the trees provide a sequence of interest through the medium of the leaves, flowers or berries. In the Winter witch hazel (*Hamamelis virginiana*), holly and dogwood (*Cornus* spp.) are effective; in the Spring and early Summer the chokeberries (*Aronia* spp.) and brambles are in flower and holly is still prominent; in the late Summer and Autumn holly, black haw (*Viburnum lentago*) and snowberry (*Symphoricarpus* spp.) are bright with berries. The herb layer also provides a sequence of interest with Spring flowering, before the canopy thickens, of bloodwort (*Sanguinaria canadensis*), Dutchman's breeches (*Dicentra cucullaria*), wood lily (*Trillium* spp.), anemone (*Anemone* spp.) and others; in the Summer when the canopy is dense, balsam (*Impatiens biflora*), nettles (*Urtica* spp.), and sanicles (*Sanicula* spp.); in the Autumn, asters (*Aster* spp.), golden rod (*Solidago ulmifolia*), and Joe Pye weed (*Eupatorium maculatum*).

Contrast over a span of many years occurs with the growth of trees planted as seedlings or standards, but in natural landscapes we are accustomed to see the continuous cycle of death and regeneration. When, however, there has been a disaster and the vegetation cover makes a fresh start in a natural landscape, the contrast over the years with some conifers can be very striking. Particularly with pinewoods, the trees are pyramidal in form when young, changing to bare trunks with a 'flat top' of branches and vegetation when mature. The groundflora, however, changes comparatively little because of the typical sand or gravel soils which are restrictive as regards the vegetation cover.

2.5. The canopy

The changes or contrasts through the seasons are not usually very dramatic when the tree canopy comprises light foliage because there is not such a difference in illumination at ground level between Winter and Summer. In these circumstances, the changing sky plays a more important role in the appearance of the landscape than it does in dense woodland. When light woodland conditions are associated with sandy soils, a pure society of bluebells sometimes develops, making only one contrast in the year at flowering time. Simple plant societies, it will be recalled, occur when the habitat conditions are unfriendly or the soils are very acid or very alkaline. They also occur temporarily in a disturbed situation, for example, where trees have been felled in a woodland, drifts of willow herb or rose bay (*Epilobium angustifolium*) or foxglove (*Digitalis purpurea*) invade the area.

The examples of plant relationships in natural landscapes are very numerous, and provide the designer with stimulating ideas for obtaining the maximum satisfaction in his planting designs. Continual observation of natural landscapes and analysing the visual qualities in the manner suggested in Chapter 8 will help to equip the designer with a sensitive approach. But planting design is also concerned with a satisfactory ecological solution in the selection of plants and in their placement in landscape.

References

[1] Tansley, A. G. (1949), *The British Isles and their Vegetation*, Vols. I and II, Cambridge University Press, Cambridge.

CHAPTER 3
Plants and their uses

In most regions the designer has available for selection in planting a large number of plant species, including natives and exotics. If his designs are for sites in several regions or even continents, the list of species available to him at one time or another is well nigh endless. It is possible to simplify or narrow down the task of selection by some form of classification or listing, which preferably should relate to the various purposes for which plants are used in designing landscape. Before such a classification or listing can be attempted, a knowledge of that part of the system in general use in scientific circles which relates to planting design is necessary (e.g. the pioneer classification of Linnaeus and the latest edition of Standardized Plant Names); this is based upon the evolution and structure in the following manner:

		the Orders	(e.g. Rosales)
divided into		the Families	(e.g. Saxifragaceae)
,,	,,	the Genera	(e.g. *Philadelphus*)
,,	,,	the Species	(e.g. *P. coronarius*)
,,	,,	the Hybrids and Varieties	(e.g. *P. coronarius 'Aureus'*

This kind of classification is also used to ensure in a legal sense that the plant which is purchased is indeed the plant which was ordered, and it represents a common language between countries for identification purposes. It does not, however, list plants in the ways they are used in planting design.

3.1. Plant lists

Many nursery catalogues and books on plants include their own system of listing which makes use of the common terminology of trees, shrubs, climbers, conifers, evergreens, ornamental grasses, types of roses, and perennials divided into groups (herbaceous, annuals, alpines, aquatics, etc.). Other plant lists which come closer to the requirements of the designer, and take into account size and appearance, have first the broad division into:

Trees, shrubs, climbers, perennials, grasses, ferns, etc.; each class is then divided into a size indication:

Tall, medium, small, low, dwarf, etc.; and a further division gives another version of the appearance:

Deciduous, broad-leaved evergreen, coniferous, etc. The 'ad hoc' kind of listing, which may vary from such descriptions as 'trees early in leaf' to 'trees with good autumn colour', is useful when there is a particular purpose in mind.

3.2. Uses and plant lists

These several kinds of listing do not fulfil the need for a list which 'relates to the various purposes for which plants are used in designing landscape'[1]. Professor Florence Robinson, when at the University of Illinois, U.S.A., prepared a listing based on the question 'what are the requirements of use?'[2]. Her listing comprised eight categories – groundcover, undercover plants, edgings, barriers, borders, specimens, accents, canopies and fillers. The suggested listing that follows takes into account the 'requirements of use', and further division of the classes, or a system of symbols, can be made to denote details like leaf colour and duration, flower colour and time of year, soil and climate limitations, etc.

1. Trees (basic planting): this section relates to the contemporary requirement in landscape design for the mass planting of large groups, plantations and woodlands, which, with the topography or landform, produce the large scale spatial arrangement of the landscape. The species

Fig. 3.1 The tree planting in this view of the countryside is the basic planting of the landscape, determining the spaces and opening up and limiting views.

selected for this group should be hardy, able to hold their own among other species, vigorous in growth, and with no difficult problems of visual relationship with other plants and elements of the landscape. Designers who respect ecological principles or the local scene are likely to include plants which are indigenous to the locality and exotics which have become established as part of the local scene (Fig. 3.1).

2. Trees (special effects): trees in this section would include those sufficiently individualistic, spectacular, or strong in character to occupy isolated positions, either because of these qualities or because they do not mix easily in a visual sense with other trees; the Cedar of Lebanon is an example of the former, and the Chilean pine or Monkey puzzle (*Araucaria araucana*) is an example of the latter. The group would also include trees which can act as 'accents' in a basic planting – a scarlet oak (*Quercus coccinea*) accenting a mixed plantation in which the dominant tree is a common oak (*Quercus robur* and *petraea*). Sometimes it is the rigid form of a tree like blue spruce (*Picea pungens glauca*) which dictates that it can only associate with other trees in a formal landscape; and sometimes it is the temporary nature of the effect, as with the so-called 'flowering trees' and those with good Autumn colour (Fig. 3.2).

3. Trees (barriers): barriers formed with plants are needed in landscapes for screening unpleasant views, for dividing up the landscape into spaces, for

Fig. 3.2 Weeping willows are familiar examples of trees which create a special effect in landscape.

Fig. 3.3 Photographs taken at the time of planting and after an interval of 4 years, during which time the screening planting has developed for this car park.

providing shelter from the wind, for protection against smoke and dust, for defining legal boundaries, and, as with all planting, for assisting in the creation of a beautiful landscape. In order to achieve these objectives, one looks for qualities of impenetrability through the medium of dense leaf or tangled twig growth, and for the ability to stand up to the forces ranged against the barrier. The emphasis in plant selection is likely to be on these qualities rather than upon appearance (Fig. 3.3).

4. Shrubs (basic planting): the use of shrubs in the mass as a basic constituent of the planting of landscapes, compared with their more traditional function of interest and decoration, is familiar to contemporary designers. It is likely that this division will need to be sub-divided into basic planting under full and partial shade, and basic planting in the open, because shrubs used in the mass are sometimes used as the under-storey of a plantation of trees and sometimes used to perform the same tasks at a smaller scale in the open as trees used for basic planting. The same qualities of hardiness and vigorous growth are appropriate as for trees fulfilling the same function, with a greater emphasis on evergreen plants (Fig. 3.4).

5. Shrubs (special effects): similar principles of selection apply to this division as for trees (special effects), but at the same time noting the need for shrubs which can produce special effects when a number are planted together (e.g. *Forsythia* spp. in profusion at flowering time). Conditions of full sky illumination are most likely to be present, but some plants accepting full and half shade should be included (Plate 3).

Fig. 3.4 Shrubs defining the boundary between a lawn and the meadow beyond, and also forming spaces in the landscape without interfering with the view.

6. Shrubs (barriers): impenetrability is essential, unless the barrier is merely for visual purposes, thus spikiness achieved by the habit of the twigs or by thorns is an advantage. Because the depth of the planting is likely to be much less than with a tree barrier, the superior effects of evergreen plants should be reflected in the list. Another matter to consider in the list is the ability of plants to accept pruning, either to control growth, and increase density, or to produce topiary effects (Fig. 3.5).

Fig. 3.5 The smaller scale of shrub planting compared with trees makes them a suitable barrier in small gardens.

7. Shrubs (edgings): the use of shrubs for edgings to footpaths, to outline beds of other kinds of plants, and to create line effects in traditional parterres is not a frequent occurrence in contemporary landscapes – not least because of the maintenance problem. The limitations on the selection of suitable plants are that they should be low in growth, dense and compact, and not prone to suckering. The common box has these qualities and is generally used for edging (Fig. 3.6).

8. Groundflora (woodland groundcover): the ability to accept shade and drip from trees and shrubs, and stand up to competition in the soil for nutrients and moisture, are essential qualities in the choice of plants which may include low growing shrubs, herbs and ferns (Fig. 3.7).

9. Groundflora (open land groundcover): grass mixtures fall into this category, but apart from the technical requirements of wear and tear for

Fig. 3.6 The box (in this case *Buxus sempervirens 'Aurea Marginata'*) is the shrub commonly used for edging flower beds and against footpaths.

Fig. 3.7 The groundflora of a deciduous wood in Spring with wood anemone (*Anemone nemorosa*) as an almost continuous carpet.

playing areas, the selection of species relates to the appearance of unmown areas, particularly with regard to the flower heads formed. A wide range of plants is available for creating visual interest at ground level, including low growing shrubs, creeping shrubs, suckering shrubs, herbs, and plants often listed as alpine or rock plants; it may be useful to divide this section into these several categories. Vigour in growth to cover the ground quickly, dense twigs and foliage, a spreading habit, and ability to increase by suckering are important qualities. With regard to appearance, colour and particularly a textural effect created by the leaves are desirable (Fig. 3.8).

Fig. 3.8 Prostrate junipers and sedums in the U.S.A. illustrate the range of plants available for groundcover planting.

10. Groundflora (herbaceous/perennial): the perennial herbs used in the traditional herbaceous border are familiar examples, although it is a mistake to consider them as only suitable for that use; they can be used in beds viewed from all sides and some species naturalize in rough grass areas. Colour and height are qualities that should be considered in making a list which gives ample scope for design purposes (Fig. 3.9).

11. Groundflora (herbaceous/annual): the use of annuals has diminished with the high cost of labour and to a certain extent from changing fashion. For exhibition or temporary plantings, annuals are effective and economical. This section could include bedding-out plants which also have the characteristic of being temporary in a planting design (Fig. 3.10).

Fig. 3.9 A herbaceous border of perennial plants which can be viewed from both sides, compared with the often seen examples planted against a wall or hedge.

Fig. 3.10 Annual sweet peas on the right of the picture were grown in this example as a border.

Fig. 3.11 Many climbing plants are effective in the Autumn with their berries exposed against the leaves, the latter forming a backcloth against the wall. The changing colour of the leaves can also be effective with deciduous species in Autumn.

12. Climbers: these plants include those used primarily for covering a wall, like the Russian vine (*Polygonum baldschuanicum*) and the Virginia creeper (*Vitis quinquefolia*); also, those used for their decorative effect in association with the colour and texture of a wall, such as climbing roses. Fruit trees can be trained against a wall for decorative effect to produce fruit in a sheltered environment (Fig. 3.11).

13. Aquatics and sub-aquatics: aquatic plants, for design purposes, are divided into species fully submerged, those with floating leaves and flowers, and the swordlike reeds, rushes and irises. The latter group also include the sub-aquatics growing in wet conditions. Plants which contribute to the oxygenation of the water are valuable in this section (Fig. 3.12).

Fig. 3.12 A typical example of planting in association with water, showing both plants with floating leaves and marginal or swamp plants.

The designer may also be concerned in the special area of indoor plants, and will take account of design principles of 'flower arrangement' as well as the principles outlined in this book.

3.3. Plant communities and land uses

The uses for which plants are selected is only one of the decisions to be made in planting design. The designer has also to consider the ecological and visual relationships of one plant with another, and with the habitat.

The least complicated environment likely to be encountered is a level plain, bounded by hills or valleys. With certain conditions of climate, soil, hydrological status and altitude, the rich flora of a high forest may be the natural vegetation. With other conditions the floristic result may be the simpler vegetation of the prairie, steppe or savannah, comprising for the most part herbs, and their arrangement in the landscape depends upon the invasive and resistance capabilities of the different species, with some influence from birds, animals and insects. The influence of one plant on another regarding illumination is less striking than in a forest, and to a certain extent is countered by the emergence of plants at different times of the year. The value of a prairie landscape to inspire a designer was evident in the work of Jens Jensen[3], although it does not seem that he used the prairie plant community as an exact model for his planting design. The example of the prairie is of a simple arrangement of plant species, but there is a growing interest in its application to landscape designs; for example, the author published a proposal for a 'prairie' garden in a local newspaper in the Mid-West of the U.S.A. in 1961, and in 1972 the Department of Landscape Architecture of the University of Wisconsin, U.S.A., was engaged in projects (such as Walden Park, Madison, Wisconsin, designed by Jodi Geiger) based upon the prairie model[4].

Associated with the prairie, steppe or savannah type of vegetation are the shrubs and small trees which occur in various places and densities. Except in places where the density is high, their influence upon the herb layer is not considerable. A similar arrangement of vegetation occurs in landscapes which have been largely denuded of vegetation by felling, fire or grazing by animals, and which attempt to return to the forest state, but are kept as open landscape with scattered trees and shrubs by grazing. Parklands, countryside favoured by hikers, and even orchards with a grass groundcover are sophisticated examples of uses of this kind of landscape pattern.

Other examples of open landscape occur on thin soils among rock outcrops, in screes at the base of mountain slopes, and as tundra vegetation in the cold climates of high altitude or at extreme northerly and southerly latitudes. In planting design, the selection and arrangement of plants for alpine or rock gardens, or for some groundcover plantings, can find inspiration from these models.

The habitat conditions are more complicated as regards plant species when topographical variations are present to modify the level plain. In the valleys, the soil and its hydrological status, the shelter, and the inclination/orientation of the slopes are likely to produce a woodland landscape, varying in itself particularly with the different inclinations and orientations. Then, within the woodland, the degree and variation of the sky illumination through the seasons has a considerable bearing upon what happens on the forest floor – whether, for example, there is a shrub and a herb layer, or only a herb layer which is visually effective just in early Spring before the deciduous trees come into leaf. Woodland landscapes are the places where the vegetation is dominant and use by people takes a secondary place. Thus, in planting design where use by people is anticipated, the tradition has been to use herb plants in the open in beds with passages and areas for walking between them, and shrubs and groundcover plants massed under trees – arrangements which presented less difficulty in designing for access by people. Nevertheless, the example of the herb layer in woodlands is an area for experiment. Shrubs have, of course, been used for special uses, like borders and hedges, but a frequent use in recent years has been to use them for dividing up landscape into spaces at a smaller scale than is accomplished with tree plantations.

References
[1] Robinson, Florence Bell (1950), *Palette of Plants*, The Garrard Press, Champaign, Illinois, U.S.A.
[2] *ibid.*
[3] Christy, Stephen F. (1976), *Landscape Architecture U.S.A.*, January, 60–66.
[4] Morrison, Darrel G. (1975), *Landscape Architecture U.S.A.*, October, 398–403.

CHAPTER 4

The appearance of plants

Everyone who is interested in plants has a general idea why he or she favours one plant compared with another; this kind of appreciation is for the whole plant, and is unlikely to be based upon a comparative list of visual characteristics. If there are generally accepted visual principles which help to explain why some different plants look well together, and others do not, then a knowledge of these principles can assist in the selection and positioning of plants in landscape on a sounder basis than mere intuition. At the outset it must be stated that the innumerable variables of time of day, weather and season make any possibility of a foolproof scientific method of selecting plants on a visual basis virtually unattainable. Nevertheless, an examination of the 'visual anatomy' of plants, and relationships based upon it, brings an additional tool for testing the intuitive selection methods which so many people adopt. Again, as with all matters concerning development of, and change to, landscape, it must be stated that all decisions on the choice of plants must be qualified by the soil, drainage and climatic conditions, and preferably taking account of the ecological basis of the landscape.

Another factor which is contrary to establishing a precise method of selection is the variety in the size and the arrangement of the branches and stems of any one species, although some plants (e.g. the poplars) frequently run true to type.

The terms 'form' and 'habit' are often used when talking about the appearance of plants. In the example of a weeping willow, the globular form created by the leaves at the extremities of the branch system is clearly observed, as also the weeping or drooping habit of the branches. But if we consider a conifer with a conical form (e.g. the oriental spruce, *Picea orientalis*), the habit of the branch system is obscured by the vegetation. If, on the other hand, we take plants like irises, or the alder which has vertical stems especially after coppicing (Chapter 2, Fig. 2.1), the habit aspect of the plant is dominant, and any mention of 'form' is unimportant. It will be helpful to attempt a definition of these two terms with respect to plants; 'habit' can be described as the direction of growth, and 'form' as the mass contained within the extremities of growth.

Fig. 4.1 A study, using a modelling technique, to illustrate the range of interest possible from the habit, or branch structure, of trees and shrubs.

4.1. Plant habit

Trees are among the larger plants used in landscape design in which the 'habit' aspect of appearance is most prominent (Fig. 4.1), while with shrubs the 'form' aspect is most characteristic, although as explained with reference to the example of the oriental spruce, the reverse is sometimes true, and examples where either 'habit' or 'form' are most prominent can be seen among herb species. When a designer is considering the visual result of planting two different plants close together, he or she should refer to their respective form and habit characteristics in the way they may or may not relate satisfactorily, and for this purpose he or she will need to be able to classify types of form and habit. The examples used in the following classification (Table 4.1) are selected from trees and shrubs commonly seen in Britain, and, in the classification of types of habit, the winter appearance is illustrated. While suggestions are made for the visual suitability of plants with particular 'habits', the other visual characteristics, like colour, will also influence the choice of plant.

Table 4.1 Classification of trees and shrubs according to habit

	Type	Example	Visual suitability
	Regular, forked and angular	Hybrid poplar (*Populus robusta*)	For formal situations where trees which are planted at equal distances should look alike.
	Irregular, forked and angular	Almond	For informal situations, in mixed plantations, and as specimens.
	Irregular, forked, angular, and multi-branched	Ash	Ditto, also especially useful for associating with smaller plants because of the reduction in scale at the extremities of the branch system.
	Tortuous	Twisted Peking willow (*Salix matsudana tortuosa*)	For situations where a very individualistic plant is appropriate in an enclosed space in the landscape.
	Multi-stemmed, horizontal	Hawthorn	For achieving quick vegetation cover.
	Multi-stemmed, vertical (possibly coppiced)	Alder	Ditto, also for associating with buildings, and for emphasis.
	Semi-pendulous	Birch	For situations where too much emphasis is to be avoided.

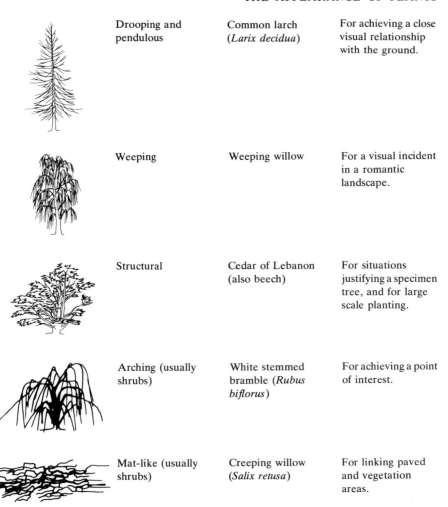

Drooping and pendulous	Common larch (*Larix decidua*)	For achieving a close visual relationship with the ground.
Weeping	Weeping willow	For a visual incident in a romantic landscape.
Structural	Cedar of Lebanon (also beech)	For situations justifying a specimen tree, and for large scale planting.
Arching (usually shrubs)	White stemmed bramble (*Rubus biflorus*)	For achieving a point of interest.
Mat-like (usually shrubs)	Creeping willow (*Salix retusa*)	For linking paved and vegetation areas.

4.2. Plant form

If we accept the definition of 'form' with respect to plants as the mass contained within the extremities of growth (Fig. 4.2), it is clear that evergreen and coniferous trees and shrubs will figure prominently, as well as deciduous trees and shrubs in the Summer, especially if they have a close cover of leaves. Some deciduous trees and shrubs also have the 'form' aspect of their appearance clearly seen in Winter if the branch and stem system is tightly arranged (e.g. the Lombardy poplar – *Populus nigra italica*). In the following classification of types of form, both coniferous and deciduous plants are illustrated as examples.

Table 4.2 Classification of trees and shrubs according to form

	Type	Example	Visual suitability
	Globular	Mulberry (*Morus alba*)	For enclosed spaces and as a specimen.
	Dome-like	Indian Bean Tree (*Catalpa bignoides*)	For association with domed buildings and with shrubs pruned to a dome-like form.
	Conical	Silver fir (*Abies alba 'Pyramidalis'*)	For use in groups, unless as an accent among other plants.
	Cylindrical	Irish yew (*Taxus baccata 'Fastigiata'*)	For giving a feeling of height to a landscape, and as a contrast to buildings with a horizontal emphasis.
	Columnar or fastigiate	Lombardy poplar	Associated with the open landscape of flat plains, and to emphasize linear elements.

	Cube	Pleached lime (*Tilia europaea*)	Associates well with a formal landscape and as a 'vegetational' extension of buildings.
	Fan-like	Walnut (*Juglans regia*)	When planted in pairs creates the arched effect of an entrance.
	Bell-like	Sassafras tree (*Sassafras albidum*)	As a specimen and for emphasizing height at the edge of woodland.
	Umbrella	Mature Scots pine (*Pinus sylvestris*)	For silhouette effect on high ground.
	Prostrate – spreading	Juniper (*Juniperus communis depressa*)	For groundcover.
	Prostrate – flat top	Juniper (*Juniperus chinensis* 'Pfitzerana')	For planting in shrub boxes.
	Prostrate – mat-like	Juniper (*Juniperus japonica*)	Ditto and for groundcover.
	Informal	False acacia (*Robinia pseudoacacia*)	Where lack of emphasis is desirable.

Fig. 4.2 A study, using a modelling technique, to illustrate the range of visual effects using plants with different combinations of branch and vegetation surfaces.

The Cedar of Lebanon, which was noted as having a structural habit, is also an example of what may be called 'open form' in contrast to 'closed form' – the latter being the usual understanding of form. The characteristic of 'open form' is seen in the separate masses of vegetation at the ends of the branch system of a mature Cedar.

4.3. Visual response to habit and form

A change in the visual effectiveness of 'form' in relation to plants occurs with distance. The eye from a considerable distance registers a silhouette effect rather than form; at middle distance the shadow effects of the vegetation masses register; at a near position the colour and texture of the vegetation have a greater visual impact than the form of the plant. These different visual effects apply more in the case of trees than shrubs and are important to note in the layout of landscape which determines the distances at which planting is observed. The distance also should influence the decision on the number of different species included in a group of trees or a woodland. The casual observer is unlikely to note as a matter of visual interest more than two different species in a group of ten trees, and in a woodland seen from the outside the inclusion of more than five or six different species is unlikely to change the impression gained. These indications of numbers of different species suitable on visual grounds will vary from one observer to another, but they should apply the brake to the planting designer's enthusiasm to complicate a planting scheme.

To the casual observer of landscape, subtle differences of habit and form are unlikely to register, but they do contribute to the many reasons why one landscape may be different from another, and this is justification for the designer to take trouble with the subtle effects achieved in the way plants are selected. Naturally, the spectacular differences between a horse chestnut (*Aesculus hippocastanum*) and a fastigiate cherry (*Prunus dulcis 'Erecta'*), if seen in relation one with another, will in all probability be noted by the casual observer.

Visual differences between plants have sometimes been illustrated by attributing human personalities to them; this has been particularly true in poetry. Just as human personalities can clash or be in harmony, so have designers and theorists suggested that certain combinations of objects which have distinctive forms or habits produce effects of stress, repose and balance. If a prostrate conifer, like *Juniperus horizontalis 'Plumosa'*, is planted alongside a shrub with a strong vertical habit, like the Russian almond (*Prunus tenella gesslerana*), some observers may have the impression of opposing forces and thus a feeling of stress. Identical plants, arranged symmetrically, give the impression of balance. And in a traditional Japanese garden the rounded forms of the clipped shrubs suggest repose (Fig. 4.3).

4.4. Colour and plants

The habit and form of a plant are the bases of its appearance, and are thus important visual factors in the way a plant contributes to the landscape.

Fig. 4.3 A Japanese garden in which the shrubs clipped to rounded forms, and the smooth grading of the ground surface, engenders a sense of repose.

Many observers of landscape, however, perceive the colour and textural effects of the flowers and leaves instead of these bases; the latter also express the slowly maturing landscape, whereas colour and texture of deciduous species mark the seasonal variations.

Colour with respect to vegetation has a very considerable range and variety in the hue or kind of colour and its density, and to these are added the variations resulting from the illumination and the nature of the leaf and flower surfaces (e.g. lustrous or iridescent). Whilst colour can be the subject of the scientific analysis of the spectrum, the simple statement of its hues – red, yellow and blue (the primary colours) and the mergings of these to give purple, orange and green (the secondary colours) – becomes complicated when these colours are 'watered down', 'shaded', mixed with the emphasis towards one colour (e.g. yellow, blue, purple, orange and green towards red), or given opacity.

4.5. Colour relationships

The spectrum, arranged as a band or circle, has interested scientists and psychologists alike to produce theories about the association of colours with one another. It should be realized, however, that in landscape the areas of different colours are not comparable with the areas covered by the different hues under any of the methods of dividing solar light; in most landscapes, there is a predominance of green or an Autumnal or Winter brown, while the other hues cover very small areas. Nevertheless, a knowledge of colour as explained by the scientist is necessary for anyone involved in planting design.

Among the primary and secondary colours of the spectrum, red, orange and yellow are associated with warmth, while blue, purple and green are regarded as cool colours. Another interpretation of this kind of perception is that the 'warm' colours appear to advance towards the observer, and the 'cool' colours to remain in the background. The pure colours of the spectrum also look closer to the observer than when tinted towards neutral grey. These perceptual effects are certainly noted by many observers, and suggest how the planting of a landscape may give a lively or a quiet sensation, and produce the effect of depth by colour emphasis on advance and recession.

A colour combination which comprises only a selection from either the 'warm' or the 'cool' colours is regarded as being harmonious, whereas the inclusion of both 'warm' and 'cool' colours produces contrast, although not necessarily disharmony. This principle of the 'warm' and the 'cool' colours has been demonstrated by arranging the spectrum as a circle (Fig. 4.4). The outer circle represents the colours at full intensity and the centre, the neutral area, represents the maximum 'tinting' or 'watering' down of the colours when it is a 'neutral white', or it can represent the maximum 'shading or darkening' to a 'neutral grey/black'. Between the outer circle and the neutral centre there is a range of intensity of spectral colour from its pure state to 'white or grey/black'. If a colour scheme is selected from the area marked 'A'

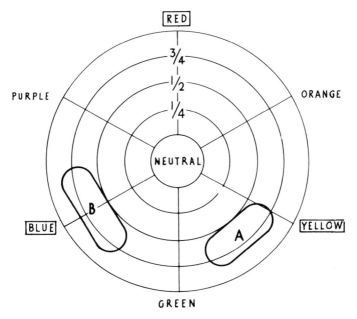

Fig. 4.4 The spectral circle.

on Fig. 4.4, the result would be harmonious, although a 'quiet' harmony with yellow modifying only towards green. If the selection is from the area marked 'B', the result would be a more 'lively' harmony because it would comprise blue (albeit in a tinted or shaded state) and colours towards purple and green.

A diagrammatic arrangement of the spectrum as a circle also draws attention to the fact that the use of opposite colours together produces an effect of contrast, e.g. red and green.

The colour circle in Fig. 4.4 is based upon three primary colours – red, yellow and blue. If, as some observers maintain, the eye recognizes four primary colours – red, yellow, green and blue – the complementary colours which produce the greatest impact, namely red and green, and blue and yellow, fall into precisely opposite places in the circle as in Fig. 4.5.

The colour circles suggest various combinations of colours. To some observers, the use of two primaries, like red and blue, with one secondary like purple, produces a strong impact, whereas two secondaries, like orange and yellow/green, with one primary, like blue, produces a more refined effect.

A variation of the colour circle based on the three primary colours is achieved by altering the position of the neutral area so that two of them, blue and yellow, are opposite in the following manner (Fig. 4.6).

The advantage of using this particular circle for colour selection is that the 'tinting or shading' variation from the pure colours is more gradual in the red range than in the green range, thus presenting another result if the selection

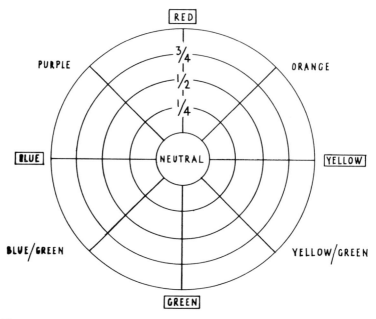

Fig. 4.5 The spectral circle based on four primary colours.

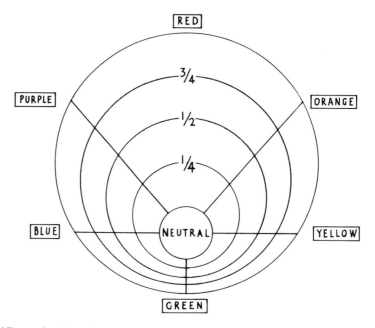

Fig. 4.6 Eccentric colour circle.

is made on a strictly geometric basis, or put in another way, the changes between blue, green and yellow and neutral 'white or grey/black' would be more sudden than the greater areas occupied by the gradual changes between purple, red and orange and the neutral area.

Another variation of the colour circle, which does not take account of 'tinting or shading', is shown in Fig. 4.7. Here, one of the colours of the spectrum is selected as the dominant and the others are changed towards the dominant by gradually increasing the effect of mixing with it. The effect of colour selection based on the dominant colour circle is harmonious.

Optical illusion is a phenomenon which has to be taken into account in selecting colours. The surroundings of an area of a particular colour, if they are grey, black, and to a lesser extent dark green, have the effect of making the colours appear brighter and larger in area. The observer's perception of a colour can also be affected by the surroundings; for example, an area coloured green looks 'more green' or intense if surrounded by a yellow area. These effects of colour relationships apply when deciduous species with light green or green/yellow foliage are planted in the edge of a coniferous forest and also in herbaceous plantings.

4.6. Colour and illumination

The perception of colour is affected by the source of illumination. A small concentrated source, such as a spotlight, gives a glossy effect, bringing out the full intensity of the colour. A large diffuse source, such as from a white ceiling illuminated by concealed lighting, tends to produce a 'satin' finish to

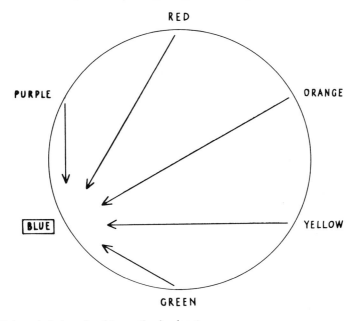

Fig. 4.7 Colour circle based on blue as the dominant.

colour, and an overcast sky produces a dull opaque effect. These effects may be explained in another way by saying that diffuse illumination desaturates colours (i.e. reduces their intensity), while directional illumination gives to colours their maximum capability in saturation or intensity. In the open, sunlight or overcast skies affect the appearance of flowers and leaves in this way, and particularly if the planting design has to take account of floodlighting at night; these differences resulting from the kind of illumination should be a factor in the selection of plant species. Yellow and yellow/green are regarded as having the greatest intensity in daylight, and blue/green at night.

The direction from which the source of illumination comes also affects the appearance of planting, especially the appearance of depth. In a planting design with several separate groups of plants spaced into the distance, the effect of distance is increased with illumination from the side. Conversely, front lighting from the position of the observer, particularly if it is diffuse lighting, gives little perception of depth. Floodlighting at night can take full advantage of the illusion of depth, but because in the day the sun varies its position hour by hour, the impact is variable, although the planting could be arranged so that this effect makes its impact in various places during the day.

The study of colour in the local and regional landscapes in which a planting design is to be drawn up is another important basis, and this should include both the humanized landscape and the plant species and their arrangement in the original natural landscape. In this respect, rectangles are drawn on a sheet of paper whose areas are approximately proportional to the areas of the different colours in a typical view and coloured accordingly, with separate sheets for the seasonal changes. Or a scenic montage incorporating the different colours of a typical scene is an alternative statement of the colours of the local and regional landscapes. From these studies, the designer has a model against which the colours resulting from his selection of, and the areas covered by, plant species can be evaluated if his or her objective is to relate new planting to the surrounding landscape. Many artists in oil and watercolour have in recent years painted landscapes in which the colour pattern is symbolized, rather than using it in an exact representation of the scene. The series of montages of the typical colours of the lower reaches of the River Tyne in North East England [1], which resulted from the River Tyne Landscape Report [2], is an example of a colour 'model' of local landscapes – to be used 'to draw the attention of all those who are in a position to influence their surroundings to the possibility of using colour so that it can make the best possible contribution to the scene.'

4.7. Planned effects

In contrast to this model of the existing colour relationships is the 'planned effect', and the simplest design is to base the planting on one colour, the most frequently observed example being green (Plate 4) in its modulation from yellow/green (e.g. lime) through green (e.g. beech) to blue/green (e.g. Italian alder, *Alnus cordata*). Using colours further removed from the pure colours of the spectrum, special effects of grey/green (e.g. willow leaved pear – *Pyrus salicifolia*) or brown/green (e.g. Japanese maple – *Acer palmatum 'Dissectum Ornatum'*) are effective. These one-colour or monocolour examples are prominent in the traditional Japanese gardens and in some sub-tropical areas with the permanent greens of broad-leaved evergreen trees and shrubs, though both have short-lived colour contrasts from the Spring blossom of cherries and azaleas and from the Autumn colours of the deciduous species. There are also many coniferous trees and shrubs which can be selected for this monocolour approach.

An alternative to green as the basic colour is the use of grey-leaved plants (Plate 5). Apart from the occasional grey-leaved tree, e.g. white poplar (*Populus alba*), their use is generally for small-scale planting, such as lavender cotton (*Santolina incana*) and rue (*Ruta graveolens*) as groundcover plants, lyme grass (*Elymus arenarius*) and southernwood (*Artemisia abrotanum*) as herbs, and *Senecio greyii* and woolly willow (*Salix lanata*) as shrubs. Most of the spectral colours combine happily with a silver/grey as a basis, including the somewhat 'chocolate box' effects of pink peonies or blue delphiniums; a quieter and effective combination is the yellow/terra cotta/brown range of everlasting flowers (*Helichrysum* var.) and grey-leaved plants.

Plants with white flowers are more effectively planted on their own among grey or grey/green leaved plants, rather than in a bed with many coloured flowers. Nevertheless, white is a 'colour' with few colour relationship problems and white flowers can enliven a planting scheme (Plate 6). Some effective examples are candytuft (*Iberis sempervirens*) as a groundcover, white larkspur (*Delphinium* var.) and Japanese anemones (*Anemone hupehensis alba*) as herbs, and *Viburnum tomentosum* as a shrub.

For planting designs where colour variety of a reticent kind is the objective, the 'watered down' colours of pink flowered plants such as some astilbes (*Astilbe 'Pink Pearl'*) and the everlasting flowers mentioned previously are typical examples (Plate 7). But when strong colour effects are required, there is ample choice from the small scarlet flowers of the Scotch creeper (*Tropaeolum speciosum*) climbing over a yew hedge to the mass effect of rhododendron species and varieties. When using plants which produce strong colour effects, the basic green of the vegetation makes them acceptable in landscape because it brings the different colours together. A plant which is effective interplanted as a moderator when the colours of the flowers of other plants tend to clash is the sage (*Salvia sclarea turkistanica*) with pale mauve flowers and conspicuous white and rose bracts.

Most of the native plants of the temperate zone which have not been hybridized produce modestly coloured flowers with few colour relationship problems. But the brilliant-coloured flowers of some sub-tropical plants require care in their use in temperate zones; in their native habitat they have to make their visual impact in strong sunlight or in the shade of evergreen forests. An example of a difficult colour relationship of this kind is the blue/red of *Rosa 'Highdownensis'* and the yellow/red *Rosa foetida 'Bicolor'*.

4.8. Plants and texture

The leaf cover of the habit and form of a plant produces a textural effect which is derived from the shape and size of the leaves, from the way in which the leaves overlap to create shadows, and from the way in which light is reflected from the leaf surface. Sometimes a plant has a thin cover of leaves so that the sky is seen through the spaces between the leaves and thus contributes to the textural effect, although this can appear as a silhouette effect when the illumination behind the plant is strong compared with that from the front.

Although textural effects have always influenced the selection of plants, the recent interest in groundcover plants, which rely almost entirely upon texture for their visual contribution, has stimulated an interest in texture in all kinds of plants.

A simple division of types of texture is into 'fine' (mown grass, Fig. 4.8), 'medium' (Privet – *Ligustrum vulgare*), and 'coarse' (rhododendrons, Fig. 4.9). A further division describes the kind of texture – 'directional' as with unmown grass or many conifers, 'geometric or patterned' as with London plane (*Platanus acerifolia*) or the pin oak (*Quercus palustris*), and 'even' as with beech. It is also proper to refer to 'scintillating' texture derived from the light reflected from the glossy surface of some leaves.

Fig. 4.8 The textural effect from a mown path through a lawn where the grass has been allowed to grow to the flowering stage.

Fig. 4.9 Some coarse textured plants are depicted here.

The size of the textural units, i.e. the leaves, gives a scale value to a plant in the same way that a wall constructed with bricks gives a different impression of size compared with a wall constructed of large stones. Thus a coarse textured plant appears closer to the observer than a fine textured plant of the same size and at the same distance. It can also be said that a coarse textured plant gives an impression of strength and stability, while a fine textured plant suggests repose; these characteristics have a significance in a large planting scheme in varied topography which gives long and short views and quiet sheltered areas.

When plants are associated with buildings and other structures, the scale of the texture also needs consideration. To take an extreme example: the large leaves of a *Magnolia grandiflora* which is growing against a brick wall produce a dull visual effect because the leaves are almost as large as the bricks. The opposite effect would be achieved by growing firethorn (*Pyracantha coccinea*) against a brick wall because of the difference in scale of the two textures which emphasizes the difference between the bricks and the living plant; there would also be the question of the particular red of the berries against the colour of the wall.

Textural differences among plants should be one of the influences in the choice of species when the following objectives are considered:

1. Giving the impression of strength in a planting scheme such as might be required at the bottom of a planted slope.
2. Creating accent effects.

47

3. Creating a background to a distinctive feature by plants with a variety of fine textures.
4. Giving interest to the smooth surface created by the leaves of a plant with a globular form.
5. Assisting to emphasize the depth of a landscape.
6. Achieving unity in a planting design by the continuation of one kind of texture through a range of plant species.

References
[1] Wakefield, L. in association with Laurie, I. C. (1969), *Colour on the Tyne,* Joint Committee of Riparian Local Authorities, c/o City Planning Department, Newcastle upon Tyne.
[2] Laurie, I. C. (1965), River Tyne Landscape Report, *ibid.*

CHAPTER 5
Visual effects with plants

Our influence upon the landscape takes two different forms, seen in the arrangement of the topography, vegetation and water to suit land uses, and in its effect on the appearance of the landscape to which planting makes no small contribution. In the natural landscape, the use aspect is the perpetuation of the habitat, while the visual effects rarely correspond with the emphasis we place on visual design matters like contrast and symmetry. But the design principles of uniformity, and particularly unity and balance are present in the natural landscape. A sign of our unique position among other living beings is our ability to transform the landscape to suit our needs, both functional and visual, but if the transformation is to be well done, the visual effects made by planting are important in the landscape design and planning process.

5.1. Uniformity and unity

Uniformity as observed in a habitat in the natural landscape is created by the repetition of a grouping of plant species in the same manner over the habitat. This arrangement may be thought to lack interest, and be unacceptable in landscape design, but interest can be provided by using a dominant plant throughout the habitat whilst varying the under storey and ground layers, or by the repetition of a particular grouping of plant species at intervals. Another solution is in the way the plants are arranged, for example, an equal spacing of trees in a regular arrangement creates a uniform effect, even if several different species are used.

Uniformity, however, may be considered a dull and uninteresting characteristic of a landscape, and a better objective is to aim for unity in planting. Unity in landscape, being defined as the coherence of its several parts and elements, provides scope for variation in the planting; this could be arranged by devising a list of plants which are visually harmonious and well related to the site conditions, and then selecting from the list so that each grouping of plants had one third of its plants in common with adjacent groups. Alternatively, a recognizable quality throughout the planting will create the effect of unity; to take a simple example, the parklands of the 18th century English School of Landscape were planted with groups of trees which were spaced at varying distances and sometimes minor changes were made in the species selected, yet these landscapes have a unified appearance and an immediately recognizable quality. Many designers have an unmistakable stamp which is evident in their work, and this personal quality can give unity to the landscape, including the planting.

Between one plant and another, uniformity means the same species. Unity, however, can be achieved by two plants having some common characteristics of form, habit, colour and texture. If two of these characteristics were present and similar in each plant of a group of between 3 and 7 different species, or one similar characteristic in each plant of a group of between 8 and 15 different species, the result would have a satisfactory degree of unity without being uniform – this is a personal opinion and some observers may feel the need for a greater degree of similarity to satisfy them in this respect.

Design in landscape necessarily takes into account the movement of the observer through the landscape. Thus, in the planting, unity can be achieved by the observer being faced every so often with similar planting effects as he moves through the landscape (Fig. 5.1). The planting can also be arranged so that the background planting is uniform, while the foreground planting

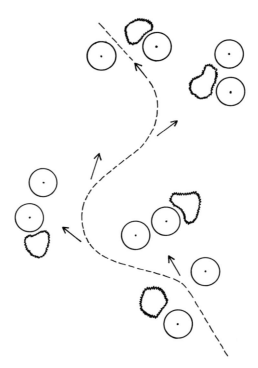

Fig. 5.1 This diagram shows how planting can be arranged so that the observer comes across similar effects as he moves through the landscape, and thus a sense of unity is created.

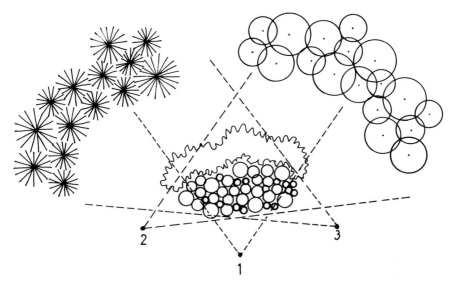

Fig. 5.2 A diagram indicating how planting can be arranged so that the planting of the foreground is constant in the observer's view, while the background can change as he moves about the landscape.

changes as the observer moves about (Fig. 5.2), or vice versa; in this example, the combination of uniformity and change results in the observer's perception of the quality of unity.

5.2. Contrast in planting

Contrast, as a conscious effect, has interested designers in every medium, and the reasons for its use include avoiding monotony, awakening the observer's interest or even shocking him or her. In planting design, the simplest arrangement to create contrast is that between adjacent areas having a woodland or shrubcover and a groundcover like grass. Within the woodland or shrubcover, contrast results from groups of coniferous and groups of deciduous species, while the management of open grassland so that part of the area is closely mown and the rest allowed to grow uncut is well known (see Fig. 4.8).

If contrast in a landscape is to be achieved through the planting of contrasting species, there are many ways of doing this, although some of them will be discarded because of their disunifying effect. The use of plants with different coloured or textured leaves and the use of plants with contrasting forms, such as 'columnar' cypresses (*Cupressus sempervirens*, Fig. 5.3) among the rounded forms of some shrub species, are examples of contrast. The comments in Chapter 4 on the use of colour in planting design for contrast suggest other ways, although these may produce disunity unless there is a basic planting with a cool and neutral colour effect and especially when grey-leaved plants are used.

51

Fig. 5.3 Contrast in the planting of a landscape through the medium of the tall cypresses 'rising' out of the rounded forms of the shrubs.

We have seen how planting which has been designed from the point of view of moving through the landscape can produce an effect of unity. In a similar way, contrasts in planting can be arranged so that the observer is suddenly faced with a different effect each time he turns a corner.

Some designers have used an approach to planting design which is based upon Japanese flower arrangement, and as a result their planting designs can embody strong contrasts and also subtlety in the way the visual characteristics of plants together produce a work of art (Fig. 5.4); but this approach runs on a different track from the ecological approach, and is best reserved for small scale planting like contrasting witch hazel with a twisted willow and again with a plant with the formal structure of the plantain lily (*Hosta sieboldiana*). Suitable places for these unecological plantings are small areas in association with the details of a building.

5.3. Symmetry and asymmetry

Symmetry and asymmetry are effects that designers create in various media; in planting design, unity and contrast can be introduced in both of them. The repetition of one plant species on each side of a centre line produces a symmetrical effect with unity, as also woodland blocks on each side of a centre line, but with contrasting species in the block. Unity in an asymmetrical layout of the planting comes from the use of one species throughout, and contrast by introducing different species for each section of the layout.

Fig. 5.4 A planting scheme at the entrance to a building which exploits the design interest of different plants at the scale associated with flower arrangement.

Planting on each side of a route is the familiar example of a symmetrical effect, and it can take various forms. For example, training fruit trees to form an arch over a path (Fig. 5.5) or the espalier treatment of fruit trees on each side, trees with a repetitive form and habit (e.g. the horse chestnut), and the exact symmetry of pleached limes. Shrubs used symmetrically in this way either form borders (Fig. 5.6) or are pruned or cut as trained hedges. Noting again the fact that landscapes are viewed by the observer moving through the landscape, false and temporary symmetrical effects are produced by arranging blocks of planting receding into the distance (Fig. 5.7) in such a way that from time to time one block appears opposite to another of apparently the same size. Symmetry is, of course, tied to a specific viewpoint, but by introducing several meeting points of radiating avenues, the historical formal garden was able to keep the idea of symmetry constantly in the perception of the observer as he walked through the landscape (Fig. 5.8). Provided the observer has an elevated viewpoint, however, symmetrical plantings of groundcover plants can be viewed from any position without losing the effect.

The creation of true symmetrical effects limits the designer, and the idea of balance is a more frequent design objective. With balance in planting design, a symmetrical effect is possible by placing groups of different species in such a way that the observer perceives some different symmetrical and some balanced effects in his perambulation through the landscape – sometimes two similar groups appear symmetrically placed and sometimes

Fig. 5.5 A symmetrical effect along a path created by trees trained as an arch.

Fig. 5.6 Trees which have been trained to repeat a conical form, and are planted equidistant on each side of a path or road, introduce a symmetrical effect.

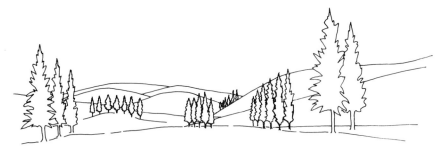

Fig. 5.7 Blocks of planting receding into the distance can produce symmetrical effects from time to time as an observer moves through the landscape.

Fig. 5.8 The ultimate in symmetry is reached in this kind of 'parterre planting'.

two dissimilar groups are balanced, and at no time is the symmetrical effect an extreme and continuous one as with an avenue (Fig. 5.9).

Balance and symmetry are also accomplished in landscape when there is a dominant centrepiece, such as a fine building. The exact matching of species and positions of the plants on each side creates symmetry, while minor variations in the planting will create balance – the more the building is visually emphatic, the less need for symmetry compared with balance in the planting.

The technical problem of growing trees and shrubs so that each plant exactly matches its fellows, and thus makes perfect symmetry possible, can be overcome by topiary or pleaching practices. A compromise between the

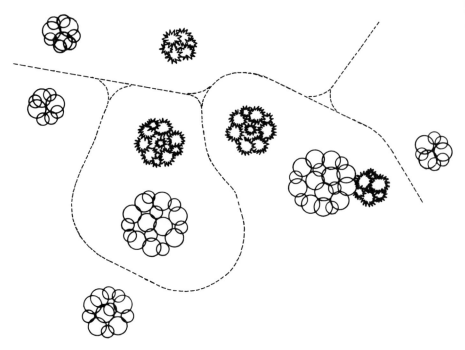

Fig. 5.9 This planting diagram shows how symmetrical and balanced effects can be created through the medium of tree groups and different species.

labour involved in these practices and planting in symmetrically located positions, but allowing natural growth, is to outline the planted areas with hedges maintained to match each other, while allowing the trees and shrubs to grow naturally behind. Another suggestion is to plant species with prominent colour, texture or form at intervals and in matching positions in the planted areas on each side of the line upon which the symmetrical effect is based, whilst adopting a less rigid approach for the planting between; the visual impact of the symmetrically planted and matching species being sufficient to satisfy the observer that the designer's objective was symmetry.

Traditionally, symmetrical planting alongside avenues took place within a short distance of the track or carriageway, with some exceptions when a wide grass verge separated the track from the trees. This arrangement can lead to the tree planting of the avenue appearing small in scale when the avenue traverses countryside with a large field pattern. If it is possible to plant the trees within the adjoining fields so that the breadth of the avenue is much greater than that of the track and verges, the avenue planting will seem to belong to the rural landscape, instead of 'piercing' it.

From the point of view of horticultural and arboricultural techniques, asymmetrical effects with planting are a simpler task, and the suggestions made previously for contrasting effects are relevant but may be considered too definite. The designer may, therefore, lessen the observer's perception of asymmetry by a design policy of planting to create balance but with some variation in the species; this policy may be considered the same as, or similar to, designing for unity.

5.4. Simplicity in planting design

In Chapter 2, the point was made that the arrangement of plants in natural landscape is usually a simple one – through a limited number of different species, through a single or very few dominant species, or through a considerable number of species extending over a large area of land as an even multi-coloured and multi-textured carpet. Simplicity in planting design is desirable when the design of the landscape has to be complicated or when the landscape is to serve as the setting for many different uses or buildings. This important principle in planting design needs always to be practised with the increasing complexity of the demands on environmental planning, and is embodied in the following suggestions:

1. Selecting the plants from one species, but using many varieties of the species – an example is a 'collection' of bearded irises.
2. Selecting plants with simple forms and habit, i.e. uncomplicated by an involved branch structure – for example, tall fastigiate trees growing through a low groundcover (in natural landscape, the successional stage of birch trees growing through heather may be noted).
3. Using one type of plant, i.e. all trees or all shrubs with a groundcover mainly of a single species (Fig. 5.10).

Fig. 5.10 An effect of simplicity is created in this landscape by planting trees with an almost bare groundcover.

4. Restricting the selection of plants to those with a common visually-emphatic characteristic – for example, plants with large leaves.
5. The commercial planting in orchards and soft fruit nurseries are examples of simplicity in planting.

The subtleties of visual effects in planting design may not be appreciated by the average observer, and the designer may feel the need to make his design more clear and emphatic in order to register. The use of contrast in the selection of plant species has been referred to and is likely to interest the less sensitive observer, and the separation of the tree, shrub and groundcover layers by selecting plants within specific height limitations, or keeping trees and shrubs separate from one another, contribute to an understanding of the designer's objective.

Arranging the planting so that the designer's intentions are more easily understood can also help to produce an effect of distance or depth in landscape, and reference to the way in which the colour of plants aids this effect was made in Chapter 4; large or coarse textured plants in the foreground of designed areas and light textured plants in the background serve a similar purpose. The stage scenery effect of receding planes painted at diminishing scales of vegetation or buildings also has the effect of distance or depth, and can be adapted to the use of planting design in landscape for this purpose. This latter suggestion has greater impact when the illumination comes from one side or other of the view.

CHAPTER 6

Landscape layout and planting

A designer plans open and closed areas in landscape in order to meet the various use requirements of his brief and to modify the local climate to suit these uses; for these purposes, the designer is likely to use plants for dividing up the landscape into sheltered open areas by means of hedges, shelter belts and the edges of woodland. The closed areas are the woodlands with their canopy of trees. Groundcover vegetation is common to both areas and gives a sense of continuity through the landscape, although on occasion hard materials like gravel take the place of vegetation. Sometimes the groundcover planting exists in its own right as a decorative feature, and may then be known as a parterre which needs provision for viewing from above in order to give the observer an adequate view (see Fig. 5.8).

6.1. Groundcover planting

Several possibilities are available for groundcover planting in its role as the medium for continuity. Grass is the most frequently planned groundcover, more frequently kept mown and less frequently allowed to grow and develop flower and seed heads; in the latter case, interest can be given by including among the grasses wild plants like yarrow (*Achillea millefolium*), the dog daisy (*Chrysanthemum leucanthemum*), the greater knapweed (*Centaurea scabiosa*), the globeflower (*Trollius europaeus*), the poppy (*Papaver lacteatum*) and the foxglove (*Digitalis lutea*), and, of course, bulbs like the wild daffodil (*Narcissus pseudo narcissus*) and bluebells in light shade (Plate 8). Some of the wild plants in grasses can be sown with the grass seed and others may need to be planted. Most of the wild herbs and bulbs suitable for growing in grassed areas are short-lived as regards visual effectiveness, but the flowering and seeding of the grasses comes later in the Summer and maintains interest in these areas. An even density of plants should be avoided in order to produce a natural effect among the grasses, and the usual recommendation for bulbs is to distribute them in 'drifts' (Fig. 6.1). There is a problem with unmown grass areas as regards access without damage, but the solution of mown grass paths is very acceptable.

There are some low growing shrub species which can mingle with unmown

Fig. 6.1 Bulbs planted in 'drifts' are one of the most common plantings to give seasonal interest to grass areas.

grass areas, for example heather species, dwarf gorse (*Ulex europaeus minor*) and the taller snowberry (*Symphoricarpus rivularis*). These plants in natural conditions often occupy sites with extreme conditions of soil acidity, thin soil and exposure, or where mature planting has been removed, and hold their own in the appropriate condition, but in more favourable conditions they are likely to be succeeded by higher forms of vegetation; thus it is wise to arrange for experimentation or for a planting plan which allows for natural selection to take place. The groundcover areas of moss species in Japanese gardens (Fig. 6.2) perform the same kind of planting function as grass areas, although they cannot withstand the same amount of use; their colour and soft texture are the envy of designers in other countries, but research has yet to be undertaken to find out if growth techniques can be successful elsewhere in mild damp climates.

In woodland conditions compared with open grassland, the likelihood of reduced wear from people and animals grazing, and the sheltered and more equable microclimate, increases the range of possible groundcover plants which will grow densely, such as ivies (*Hedera* spp.), ferns, early flowering herbs like wood anemone and Winter aconite (*Eranthis hyemalis*). The innovation of the woodland garden in the 19th century included the planting of many species which served as groundcover plants, the result being a more varied groundcover than in the natural woodland. There are also slopes in open landscape which may suggest planting stonecrops (*Sedum* spp.) or sea thrift (*Armeria maritima*) among stones to create the effect of a scree or cliff top near the coast (Fig. 6.3).

Fig. 6.2 Mosses as groundcover are typical of many Japanese gardens.

Fig. 6.3 A garden in the U.S.A. formed on a slope with the design of the landscape based on a scree, and planted accordingly.

61

When groundcover plants are used on their own as a decorative feature, the range is considerable, and the design principles already stated in regard to colour and texture need to be followed in order to arrive at a successful result. But if groundcover planting is designed to give continuity over the whole area of the landscape, the number of species is best limited to three or four in order to emphasize the idea of continuity and to avoid competing with the rest of the planting.

Over the years, decorative groundcover planting has taken several forms, the best known being the parterre in its geometric and floral patterns; this has a long history in many countries and has had several revivals (Fig. 5.8). Materials like earths and gravels were sometimes used in association with the plants, and the pattern was also produced by an edging or outlining plant like box. Each of the several forms necessitates considerable maintenance which influenced designers to adopt a less definite pattern, allowing the areas covered with different plants to grow into one another so that the result is the effect of a painting made by applying colour and allowing it to run freely (Fig. 6.4). These less definite patterns offer scope for the use of shrubs like prostrate junipers or the prostrate cotoneaster (*Cotoneaster dammeri*) to be used with perennials like stonecrops or sweet williams (*Dianthus barbatus* var.).

Some recent designers of decorative groundcover planting (e.g. Burle Marx – see Section 1.6) have taken as their model the abstract patterns associated with the paintings of some artists; these designs in common with geometric and floral patterning require considerable maintenance in order

Fig. 6.4 Groundcover planting with tufted grasses (*Festuca glauca*) and sedums, relieved by dwarf conifers.

to keep the pattern exactly as designed; the edging or outlining technique with a low and slowly growing shrub, alternating the planting with hard surfaces, and vertical obstructions to root growth in the soil are methods used to reduce the maintenance problem. It is also wise to select plants with a slow growth and especially avoiding plants with a strong tendency for suckering if it is important that the original design is to remain. A familiar alternative for keeping the design intact is by means of the annual bedding-out technique, using plants propagated in a nursery, and adopted for floral clocks and coats of arms in public places, but this technique is also labour intensive. Examples of plants which are not too difficult to keep within limited areas are the houseleek (*Sempervivum tectorum*) and the sea thrift.

The Winter appearance of groundcover areas is a cause for concern when many perennial plants lose their leaves in that season. A carefully thought out pattern may not, however, suffer if bare soil takes the place of vegetation during the Winter. The yarrow (*Achillea tomentosa*) and some stonecrops (e.g. *Sedum spurium roseum*) sometimes retain a basal rosette of leaves through the Winter, and shrubs like periwinkle (*Vinca minor*) and the wintergreen (*Gaultheria procumbens*) are evergreen. The possiblity of a different appearance in the Winter draws attention to selecting the plant species so that the design provides for a changing appearance throughout the year with various species coming into flower at different times.

The initial and the early maintenance, or rather development, costs can be high for groundcover areas. If the plants are small, a large number will need to be planted at about 300 mm centres; if the spacing is based upon the diameter of large plants at maturity, for example the sargent juniper (*Juniperus chinensis sargentii*), it would be between 2 and 3 m, but this necessitates a succession of weeding operations over a long period until the gaps close up. Techniques like covering the ground with black plastic sheets with holes for each plant or a layer of mulch can reduce the growth of weeds.

6.2. Planting and spaces

Plants are the most frequently used medium for creating spaces in landscape for various purposes like sitting areas in private gardens, stage entertainments in city parks, and sheltered fields for agriculture and horticulture (Fig. 6.5). If the space is large and crosses an ecological boundary, the question arises as to whether the species should change when the boundary changes or should remain on the premise that the space formed is a unit and this fact should be reflected in the enclosing medium. When the spaces are small, the designer's skill may be able to make the spaces fit the ecological pattern of the natural landscape, and thus the problem of planting different species along a single hedge or belt of trees will not arise. But when the spaces are large and cross ecological boundaries, one selection would be a species able to flourish in the different conditions, assuming competition from other species is checked; another selection

Fig. 6.5 Shrub and tree planting in Holland creating spaces in a recreational landscape (courtesy of Ian C. Laurie).

would be several species likely to survive all the conditions as a mixture and with time as the decision-maker on survival. If the designer is primarily interested in the abstract or the formal nature of his design, paying little heed to the ecological pattern of the natural landscape, he is likely to select a single species because this will emphasize his design and avoid the distracting influence of species variety in the enclosing medium. Under conditions where there is a shortage of groundwater as in arid landscapes, artificial irrigation channels would be necessary for the planting which creates the spaces, and this would relate the species to the water supply, resulting in uniformity.

A different approach to planting design with the purpose of creating spaces in landscape is to assume that a forest or woodland exists over the entire area, followed by clearances to create the spaces for various purposes. This approach is very appropriate for the forest park type of recreational area.

The designer may wish to have a visual link as the observer moves from one space to another by means of his selection of plant species to give continuity whilst giving identity to each space (Fig. 6.6). Alternatively, each place where the observer moves from one space to another can be marked by a concentration of one species, and if this species is also planted at intervals through all the spaces it will act like a dominant able to override minor changes in soil conditions, and these latter can be reflected in changes in the rest of the planting.

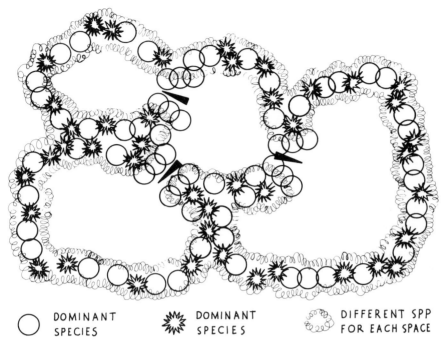

<table>
<tr><td>○ DOMINANT SPECIES</td><td>✳ DOMINANT SPECIES</td><td>≈ DIFFERENT SPP FOR EACH SPACE</td></tr>
</table>

Fig. 6.6 In this planting design for creating spaces, the dominant tree species are the same around each space, with a concentration of one species as the observer moves from one space to another. The shrubs and groundcover under the trees are varied to give each space an identity without disturbing the landscape as a whole.

Traditionally, planting for creating spaces in landscape has been uniform, using plants which can be trained to conform to a standard height and appearance by pruning, clipping or pleaching techniques; for example, the cypress (*Cupressus macrocarpa*), yew, beech, hornbeam (*Carpinus betulus*) and lime. Some species like Lombardy poplars and the Irish yew (*Taxus baccata 'Fastigiata'*) produce a uniform appearance without applied techniques, but their respective heights have to be accepted. Poplar trees in various species and varieties are, of course, used in Northern Europe for creating spaces in agricultural landscape. In Britain, the spaces were traditionally created by hedgerow species using hawthorn, with some planted and some natural variations like blackthorn (*Prunus spinosa*) and wild roses (e.g. *Rosa canina*), and by shelter belts and woodlands of various tree species.

At the smaller garden scale, many different species have been selected for creating spaces besides the familiar examples of cypress, yew, beech and hornbeam. The mixed shrub border, tall grasses (e.g. *Miscanthus sinensis*), bamboo (e.g. *Arundinaria fastuosa*; Fig. 6.7) and some reed species in damp conditions (e.g. *Typha angustifolia*) give particular qualities to a space. Polyantha roses and *Escallonia 'Donard Star'* give yet another quality to a

Fig. 6.7 Bamboos in the centre of the picture are useful for enclosing spaces when the conditions are suitable – their numerous stems forming a screen.

space. The technique of building a frame for climbing plants is also sometimes used for enclosing space in gardens.

When selecting plants for enclosing space, the designer will need to consider the height of the plants in relation to the size of the space. To some observers, a tall beech hedge 4 m high, enclosing a space 10 m wide, may be oppressive, while a layered hawthorn hedge 2 m high around a large field 400 m wide may be insignificant compared with a hawthorn hedge which has been allowed to grow untrained to a height of 6 m. The designer will also need to consider the detail of the planting in relation to the size and use of the space; there are no rules on this matter, but the reader may like to form his own judgement on the following sizes of spaces beyond which the types of plants listed lose their individuality and thus their contribution to the visual impact that the particular species make in the space:

Perennials	30 to 50 m across
Small shrubs and tall grasses	50 to 60 m across
Large shrubs and bamboos	60 to 100 m across
Small trees	100 to 150 m across
Large trees	150 to 200 m across

Note: most of the observation in the spaces is likely to be at places within the middle third of the distances listed.

The visual effect of the height of plants upon the space they enclose can be to diminish or increase its apparent size; thus tall trees surrounding a small space emphasize its small size, and conversely small shrubs around a large space make an indefinite boundary.

Spaces in landscape are not two-dimensional, although the fact that they are generally open to the sky can give this impression. It is possible to use plants to break up the volume of spaces without actually dividing them and thus draw attention the third dimension of the spaces (Fig. 6.8). A most effective tree in this respect is the American elm (*Ulmus americana*) when planted so that two or more trees are so spaced that their crowns link, creating the effect of the ribs of a Gothic vaulted roof without the solid infilling – sadly this type of planting has been severely hit by disease.

6.3. Planted screens

The use of plants to form screens in the landscape has much in common with the comments on their use for enclosing spaces, but the emphasis is likely to be on screening for privacy or hiding something which is objectionable. If it is an unsightly object or view, the aim will be to select plants that will grow quickly, while the matter of overcoming any 'seeing through' effect will be solved either by the width of the screen or its density. Quick-growing trees like willows and poplars, and shrubs like forsythia (*Forsythia intermedia*) and quince (*Chaenomeles speciosa*) are familiar choices when complete all-the-year screening is not required. But for maximum and permanent screening, species with dense and evergreen foliage are necessary, for

Fig. 6.8 The tracery of the branch and twig system of a beech tree gives the third dimension to a space in landscape.

example, trees like *Cupressocypari leylandii* and spruce (*Picea excelsa*), and shrubs like Portugal laurel (*Prunus lusitanica*) and the common rhododendron (*Rhododendron ponticum*). Screening for noise by means of vegetation is less effective than visual screening, but tests have singled out the sycamore when in leaf and the shrub *Viburnum rhytidophyllum* throughout the year as the most beneficial, depending upon the height of the source of the noise[1]. The selection of plants for screening purposes requires a study of the topography and the distances between the observer and the place or object to be screened; this information has to be related to the height that the selected plants are likely to achieve within a period understood by all concerned.

6.4. Planted backgrounds

Planted screens, hedges and tree belts give scale, shelter and interest to a landscape, but they can also form the background to another type of planting or to an artefact. When the objective of the planting is to serve as a background, some consideration should be given to the selection of plants regarding visual competition between the foreground and the background, the normal objective being that the latter should not dominate the former. Thus, plants selected for background effects should not have too great an individuality, and if they can create the illusion of distance, this is an advantage. Plants which have one or more of the following characteristics fall into this category:

1. Those with pale coloured leaves (e.g. white willow – *Salix alba*, sea buckthorn – *Hippophae rhamnoides*, and *Elaeagnus angustifolia*).
2. Those with a fine leaf texture (e.g. birch, barberry – *Berberis darwinii*, and *Sophora viciifolia*).
3. Those with a graceful and light branch habit (e.g. larch, mock orange – *Philadelphus coronarius*, and *Buddleia alternifolia*).

Although contrary to the principles outlined, the occasional planting of a few conspicuous trees or shrubs among the mass of the background planting can have the effect of increasing the apparent distance to the background. And using plants with strong Autumn or Spring colour effects can provide temporary variety in the landscape by enabling the background to become the foreground for short periods.

When an artefact, for which the background planting is to be selected, has considerable detailed interest, such as a sculpture or a highly articulated Gothic facade, the plants should have an even colour and texture so that there is no competition as to detail (Fig. 6.9) – a sculpture in front of a clipped yew hedge, for example. If, however, the artefact is a Regency stucco building with few delicate details, the scene could be enlivened with a background of varying colours and textures. Perhaps with this in mind, designers have felt the need to create a background to the smooth surface of a lake.

Fig. 6.9 The even texture of the trees, forming the background to the building, does not compete with it.

The design of the plan shape, the silhouette, and the placement of a background in a landscape is a difficult task because rarely are the foreground and background restricted to one viewpoint. When the background can extend around three sides of the foreground, the view is limited and the foreground/background relationship can be designed with a definite viewpoint in mind.

An important visual task of background planting is that of unifying a complicated foreground planting design like a parterre or a herbaceous border. In fact, background planting frequently performs the two tasks of providing a background and giving unity and visual continuity to a landscape.

References

[1] Beck, Gerhard, 1965, *Pflanzen als Mittel zur Lärmbekämpfung*, Patzer-Verlag GMBH and Co., K.G., Hanover.

CHAPTER 7

Grouping plants

In previous chapters reference was made to the visual analysis of individual plants and to some visual principles influencing the ways in which different plants may or may not relate well in adjacent positions, and this leads on to the consideration of plant relationships in groupings. In natural landscapes there are some instances where each type of plant (trees, shrubs, herbs and other groundcovers) grows almost in isolation, such as coniferous forests, low fertility slopes, prairies, and tundra. The more usual natural plant community of the developed and underdeveloped areas met in landscape design has the complete range of plants in a close physical relationship – such as a rich woodland community. The designer, however, may find it necessary for practical and aesthetic reasons to vary this relationship, sometimes contrasting shrub areas with herb areas, or trees with groundcover plants.

7.1. Types of groups

The grouping of plants of one type or several types is associated with familiar descriptions which have no precise size in numbers or area, and indeed not very precise definitions, although the following groupings and suggested number of plants or areas may be helpful:

A group of trees	from 3 to 10 trees
A large group of trees	from 11 to 20 trees
A clump of trees (a compact planting, often oval or circular in plan)	from 11 to 20 trees
A copse or coppice (originally dominated by coppiced trees, but with some undergrowth)	more than 20 trees
A spinney or thicket (with dense undergrowth and possibly established as a game habitat)	more than 20 trees
A wood (natural or planted)	1.2 or more hectares
A plantation (specifically planted)	1.2 or more hectares
A grove (scattered trees with open areas)	2.0 or more hectares

These groupings nearly always relate to trees as the visual dominant, and

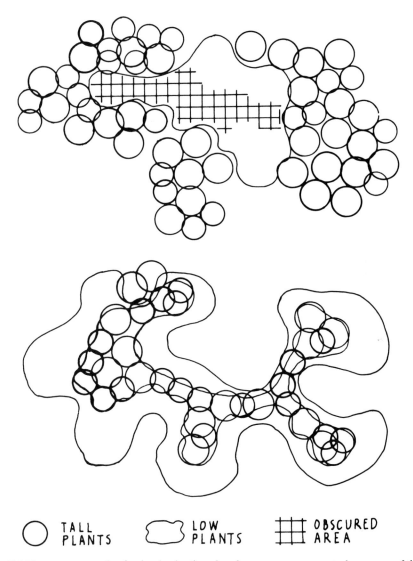

TALL PLANTS   LOW PLANTS   OBSCURED AREA

Fig. 7.1 The upper example of a simple planting plan shows an arrangement where some of the planting is obscured, compared with the lower example where all the planting is easily visible.

there is no equivalent for the other types of plant, except reference is made to a group of shrubs, a bed or a border of shrubs or perennials, or an area of groundcover plants.

The ways in which plants are grouped should include the practical considerations of covering the ground in order to limit maintenance and to control erosion, as well as for use by people. A practical consideration from the point of view of appearance is to arrange the plants in a group so that their visual effectiveness is apparent, which is important to the client who

71

has to meet the cost. Thus, the designer considers whether a group should be seen from only one side or from all round, and how the kinds of plants and the width across the group may lead to some of them being hidden from view (Fig. 7.1).

7.2. Natural groupings

A grouping of trees, shrubs, herbs and groundcover plants which is close to a typical arrangement in natural landscape is shown in Fig. 7.2; the trees are grouped so that there are some areas without a canopy, and thus with good illumination. In these open areas, the herbs (represented by beds of perennials) thrive in the good illumination and in the sheltered microclimate provided by the shrubs; the herbs also benefit from the visual enclosure and background effect of the shrubs. The groundcover plants, selected for their

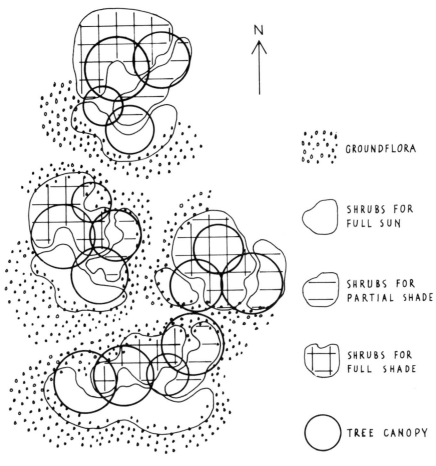

N

GROUNDFLORA

SHRUBS FOR FULL SUN

SHRUBS FOR PARTIAL SHADE

SHRUBS FOR FULL SHADE

TREE CANOPY

Fig. 7.2 An example of a planting scheme based upon the arrangement of plants in a natural woodland, but with spaces for use and observation.

ability to withstand shade and drip, are located under the trees, and the shrubs link the open and canopied areas with the selection of species varying from those able to withstand shade to those requiring good illumination.

A grouping of the four different types of plants can be given coherence by emphasizing the height differences of the four layers of strata, selecting plants likely to grow to a particular height. This somewhat rigid approach can be varied by accentuating the layering effect in one or two types of plants, while arranging a variety of heights in the other types.

7.3. Visual effects

When two types of planting are grouped together, such as a shrub edge to woodland or perennials receding into alcoves in a shrub background, the visual result is more effective if plants of the two types do not produce their flowers at the same time, otherwise the effect of setting one type against another will be reduced – this is not easy to achieve because so many 'flowering' trees and shrubs produce their flowers at the same time in Spring or early Summer, and the Autumn colour period is even more likely to occur at the same time.

The designer will need to consider in grouping plants the amount of planting of one type compared with another type. A landscape small in area which has equal areas devoted to each of the four types – trees, shrubs, herbs and groundcovers – is likely to lack visual effectiveness, but if the area is large the areas can be the same provided the proportions vary from one part of the landscape to another. If, however, the plants are selected to produce colour and textural variation, some observers may not consider that equality in area lacks interest. Selecting coniferous species for one type of planting and deciduous for another also overcomes visual monotony when equal areas are devoted to the different types of plant, and is often equally effective in the Winter when deciduous species with interesting branch systems combine with coniferous or evergreen shrubs.

These suggestions on avoiding visual monotony should, however, be qualified by considering how types of plants grow together in natural landscape and how landscape is the basis of the environment in which many different kinds of development take place. Thus, the more exciting effects which can be arranged in other disciplines are not necessarily appropriate for the unique position of the landscape as the basis upon and in which all development takes place. Plant groupings which accord with this concept are shown in Fig. 7.3, where the outline of each group suggests that it is a detached part of the adjoining groups; the analogy of a jigsaw puzzle which has been pulled apart helps to explain this planting design (Fig. 7.4). Selecting the same species for planting in each group also helps to emphasize landscape as the basis of the environment.

It can be argued that there is little need to take special care over the outline on plan of a group of plants because the vegetation is contained within the silhouette rather than by the plan shape, and the varying surface

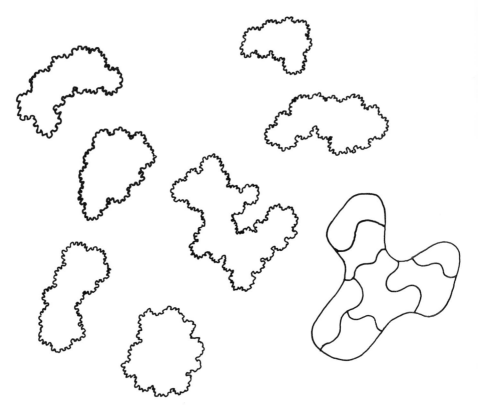

Fig. 7.3 Plant groupings which are based upon the separation of elements of one larger group shown in the diagram at the lower right of the illustration.

of the vegetation of most plants produces a varying shade patterning. In the early years of the 18th century in England, the designers used a circular or oval plan shape for their tree groups which would have been identifiable when the trees were young, but became blurred as the trees matured with some variety in the form of the vegetation. If, however, the designer's intention is that the outline of a group on plan should be recognizable by an observer, the plants should present an even surface, either through an even quality in the leaf surface or by regularly spaced trees or shrubs in the group, preferably with a vertical habit.

The manner in which the position of plants is designed in a group or border is particularly important in the first years after planting, because the main stems or trunks are very prominent until the side branches and the vegetation develop. Thus, formal planting on a grid means that, from most viewpoints, the plants in front of the observer are in line (Fig. 7.5). Preferably, the position of most plants should be diverted on either side of the grid so that from every viewpoint there are no visual passages through the plants.

Fig. 7.4 Plant groupings which may appear arbitrary until closer investigation shows how they relate to one another in a linear and an angular sense.

7.4. Visual principles

The selection of species and their arrangement within a group should be governed by the design policy for the whole landscape. Nevertheless, there are some observations which can be made about the visual relationship of the plants in a group, although they should not be taken as strict rules, always to be followed.

If a group of trees or shrubs comprises mostly conifers or evergreen species, the inclusion of one or two deciduous plants is preferable when they are within, rather than on the edge of, the group where in Winter the impression may be given of a gap in the unity of the group. The converse of a group of deciduous species does, however, seem better able to accept one or two conifers on the periphery – in Winter they will make an interesting contrast to the network of bare branches.

The size of a group has a bearing upon the number of species (see Section 5.1); for example, in a large group of 20 trees or shrubs, a mixture of

Fig. 7.5 This picture shows how by walking around the grouping of newly planted trees the observer sees the trees from time to time in a straight line. In a large plantation of this kind, the straight lines and corridors detract from the completeness of the planting unless some divergence from straight lines is arranged.

deciduous, evergreen and coniferous species can be visually successful, although restricting the number of different species is important. But in a small group of say 6 plants, the effect is not successful if there are only two species, very different in appearance and planted in equal numbers – sycamore and birch illustrate this observation. As a general rule designers in several media favour an odd number of elements which are alike. Thus, tree groups comprising one species should, on these grounds, have odd numbers of plants. If one plant is very different in appearance from the rest in a group, the result is often more successful if it is planted slightly detached from the group. There are, however, successful groups in which trees of a fastigiate form have been planted among trees of rounded forms, particularly when the fastigiate trees are in the centre of the group with the rest of the trees around growing to a lower height; if the spacing is such that glimpses are possible of the entire height of the fastigiate trees, the visual result is even better, but in general there should be a slight intermingling of the extremities of the branches of trees in a group with perhaps the occasional gap achieved by planting at a wider spacing.

Small groups of trees achieve their greatest visual interest when the centre is higher than the periphery, and this is true to a lesser degree with shrubs. There is, in any case, a tendency for this effect to happen naturally because the plants in the centre strive to reach the light. With large groups, some variation in the height over the whole canopy is acceptable, unless the aim is to produce a very formal landscape, relying entirely upon the mass effect of one species; otherwise a well chosen and reticent selection of species to give some variation in height is usually acceptable, particularly when the topography is flat.

7.5. Herbs and perennials

Groups of trees and shrubs usually help to form the spaces and divisions of a landscape, but herbs or perennials are occasionally planted for this purpose instead of their more familiar role as decorative incidents. If, however, herbs or perennials are designed to form part of the structure of a landscape, the characteristics sought in the plants will be growth to heights well above the average, dense vegetation, and the ability to remain effective for the greater part of the year, even if the leaves remain in position after the dying down. There are not many plants in temperate zones which meet these conditions, but pampas grass (*Gynerium argenteum*) in mild localities and bunch grass (*Elymus condensatus*) are examples. The larger Helleborus species (*H. orientalis* var. *colchicus*) is an example if the landscape is small in size and scale and the area of vision limited.

When herbs or perennials are planted in groups for the more frequent reason of decorative effect there is always the problem of the appearance in the off season. One solution is to design the shape of groups at ground level to form a recognizable pattern of bare earth outlined by grass or some hard surface material. Another solution is to interplant within the groups species which retain some vegetation in the off season, such as evergreen groundcover plants or the *Helleborus* species.

Isolated groups of herbs or perennials, compared with a herbaceous border linked to the landscape by a backing hedge or an adjacent footpath or wall, are more effective if the planting is restricted to varieties of a species or a few species of a family which have visual similarities; for example, a bed of varieties of flag irises is a significant element in the landscape but having variety from the different colours, and various peony species from the genus *Paeonia* are similarly effective. If the typical mixture of plants of a herbaceous border is used for an isolated group, the visual result is unlikely to be a significant element in the structure of the landscape.

7.6. Roses and grouping

Species, hybrids and varieties of the genus *Rosa* have a popular appeal which does not always accord with accepted landscape design principles, and the designer will inevitably be faced with the problem of accommodating them in groupings in his design. The 'species' roses or cultivated wild roses, and the bush hybrids and varieties closely related to them, can be considered along with shrubs and grouped in accordance with the principles outlined for shrub groupings. The hybrid tea roses, however, are a special problem. Whether or not they are pruned down to barren stumps before or after

Fig. 7.6 Low box edging hiding the unsightly results of pruning operations on hybrid tea roses.

mid-Winter matters little in their poor appearance as plants contributing to the structure of the landscape. This problem must often have been the reason why hybrid tea roses were often grown in a formal rose garden with a visually effective pattern formed by the paths or paving. If hybrid tea rose beds are edged with a low hedge, such as box, about 500 mm high, the untidy low branch structure is partly obscured (Fig. 7.6). There is also the possibility of interplanting with perennials to hide the poor branch system, but the perennials selected should not compete visually with the roses – *Salvia sclarea bracteata* and *Artemesia lactiflora* are examples of plants with quiet coloured flowers.

J. C. Loudon [1] in the Introduction to his edition of Humphrey Repton's works commented on plant groupings in the following manner:

According to the practice of Kent and Repton, and, more especially, to that of all the followers of the Picturesque School, trees, shrubs, and flowers were indiscriminately mixed, and crowded together, in shrubberies and other plantations; and they were generally left to grow up and destroy one another, as they would have done in a natural forest; the weaker becoming stunted, or distorted, in such a manner as to give no idea of their natural forms and dimensions; though forming picturesque groups and masses highly pleasing to the admirers of natural landscape. According to the Gardenesque School, on the contrary, all the trees and shrubs planted are arranged in regard to their kinds and dimensions; and they are planted at, or as they grow, thinned out to, such distances apart as may best display the natural form and habit of each: while, at the same time, in a general point of view, unity of expression and character are aimed at, and attained, as effectually as they were under any other

School. In short, the aim of the Gardenesque is to add, to the acknowledged charms of the Repton School, all those which the sciences of gardening and botany, in their present advanced state, are capable of producing.

References
[1] Loudon, J. C. (1840), *The Landscape Gardening and Landscape Architecture of the late Humphrey Repton Esq.*, Longman and Co. and A. & C. Black, Edinburgh.

CHAPTER 8

Planting design and ecology

There are two ways in which ecology serves as a basis for planting design. It is possible to make a survey of the natural vegetation when present or a conjectural analysis of it when not present and to design the planting on this basis. But it is also possible to accept the principles underlying the existence of the flora and fauna in a habitat and to use these principles for design purposes while introducing man as a new and possibly dominant factor – from either the aesthetic or use points of view, or both. Either way, the principles are important.

There is another approach to planting design in which the plants are selected in accordance with the soil, climate, aspect and other relevant environmental determinants, and for their appearance, in the knowledge that if competition from other plants is removed as a result of maintenance techniques, success is likely. With this approach the selected plants may not necessarily be based upon ecological principles.

8.1. The biotic community

The fact that the landscape is the embodiment of the influences of the flora and fauna and the habitat upon one another reminds the designer that animals, birds and insects required consideration as well as the plants and the physical conditions of the habitat; it is not sufficient, for example, to plant *Buddleia* species and varieties for encouraging butterflies into a landscape – nettles and other suitable plants are needed for the larvae to feed from[1]. Thus, the plants in an ecologically based design should be selected in the way they will contribute to a biotic rather than a plant community, and in turn, each biotic community should be able to reside congenially in the habitat, even when man exerts a major influence by his activities or his landscape maintenance methods.

8.2. Cover and food bondage

The principle of cover bondage in a biotic community refers to the link between the dominant plant and the habitat; the latter must satisfy all the requirements of the former if the link is satisfactory. The dominant plant

80

cover then modifies the habitat to produce niches or varying conditions in which the lesser plants can survive. If we consider this principle as an aid to planting design, we are faced with the nearly impossible situation of creating through the planting design the final pattern of conditions in one operation. In order to overcome this difficulty, it follows that the planting design must be closer to the sequence of evolution that Nature follows in taking over the bare soil of a virgin landscape.

Food bondage is a three-way link between the flora and fauna and the habitat. The fauna, although mobile, are tied to the habitat through the food produced by the flora and sometimes from among themselves, and the flora are tied to the habitat by immobility. In turn, the habitat relies upon the flora and fauna to replenish soil fertility.

Cover and food bondage explain the self-maintenance characteristic of an ecological basis to planting design, but, just as in a community of human beings, there is present the element of competition between species. The disastrous results which could come from competition are checked by the fact that much of the competition is predatory – one animal, whose feeding habits might eliminate a species of plant, is checked by the attacks made on it by another animal. The end result of these bondage and competitive events produces a state of balance and stability, provided the habitat and climatic conditions do not change.

8.3. The dominant species

Frequently in natural landscape there are large areas of the same kinds of flora and fauna, and these areas are recognized as communities. Also, the change from one area to another is by way of a transition zone, known as an ecotone, which can be expressed in a planting design as an area in which there could be flexibility in the choice of species from time to time. If, however, the designer's intention is to bring unity to a landscape which spans several different habitats, the selection of a dominant species over the whole landscape will achieve this result; in such a case, he or she will look for a euryvalent species which can survive over the range of different habitats. Conversely, if he wishes to identify in a definite manner the visual differences between habitats, he will look for stenovalent species, which are limited to a narrow range of physical conditions.

The most important principle which should influence the designer is seen in the link between the dominant species and the habitat; this requires precision in the selection of the dominant and, in all probability, the setting-up of maintenance operations by man until the dominant has achieved a secure position. When a long-term plan of operations is set up, a phased planting plan can be written into it, incorporating a succession of seral dominants – each one modifying the habitat so that the next dominant is favoured, until a climax situation is reached. The initial phase is marked by the emergence in a natural situation, or the planting in a designed situation, of pioneer plants.

8.4. Planting design methods

With these principles in mind, it is possible to suggest some ways in which planting design can be based upon ecology. Whichever way is chosen, a knowledge of the biotic community or communities appertaining to the site is very necessary. On the rare occasions in developed countries when the site is a natural landscape, it is a simple matter to acquire this knowledge. But when the natural landscape no longer exists through some land use, a reconstruction based upon historical data including pollen analysis and other scientific aids, and other sites with similar physical and climatic conditions, can fill the gap with the expertise of the ecologist.

A planting design which follows closely the pattern of the natural vegetation would produce in an area which is naturally forest, a landscape comprising a forest with cleared or thinned places for specific uses. A natural grassland landscape would suggest an open landscape with substantial shrub groups in place of the typical scattered shrubs. The sustaining of these changed landscapes in their new guise would depend upon maintenance operations or the control resulting from the uses of the landscape.

The brief for many landscape designs will rule out such a close similarity with the natural landscape, and other ways of using ecology as a basis have to be found. The design objectives of simplification and clarification can be applied to the arrangement or pattern of the natural vegetation. This involves a study of the two- and three-dimensional ways in which the texture and colour are arranged, and identifying the major areas of visual impact while omitting small variations; thus, the basis of the arrangement of the plants becomes clear (Figs. 8.1 and 8.2). The design of the planting then follows the simplified arrangement with a larger proportion of those species which contributed most to the texture and colour effects. The study or analysis of the natural vegetation involves plotting a typical distribution of the plants, with horizontal sections or plans through the vegetation at different levels and taken parallel with the ground; these will show the patterns of the groundcovers and of the rest of the vegetation at different levels. Typical vertical sections should also be plotted. These sections should be marked with the textural and colour differences. The analysis is then made by simplification to emphasize the main features of the patterns. Even if the analysis is not used as the model for the planting design (Fig. 8.3), the designer has familiarized himself, or herself, with the appearance of the structure of the native vegetation.

Any change from the arrangement of plants in a natural landscape does, of course, suggest that some form of control has to be exercised, but a planting design which is close to that natural to the area has a greater chance of success in terms of growth and maintenance than an 'introduced' planting design (Fig. 8.4). This particular approach to planting design can accept many variations, such as leaving out the sub-dominant species (when present in the natural landscape) to emphasize the effect of stratification in the several layers of vegetation. Also, a lesser number of different

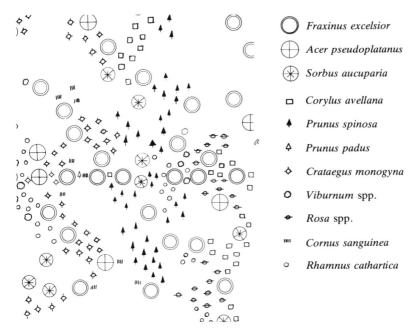

◯	*Fraxinus excelsior*
⊕	*Acer pseudoplatanus*
✳	*Sorbus aucuparia*
◻	*Corylus avellana*
▲	*Prunus spinosa*
△	*Prunus padus*
◇	*Crataegus monogyna*
◌	*Viburnum* spp.
✦	*Rosa* spp.
◺	*Cornus sanguinea*
○	*Rhamnus cathartica*

Fig. 8.1 (above) The positions of the trunks and stems of the trees and shrubs of a typical area of a natural community, based on the Ash tree as the dominant, on a carboniferous limestone formation. The area covered in the plan is 50×39 m.
(below) An analysis of the major textural effects of the vegetation of the trees and shrubs of the natural community. Similar analyses can be made of the colour effects, and these can also be made on typical vertical sections through the community.

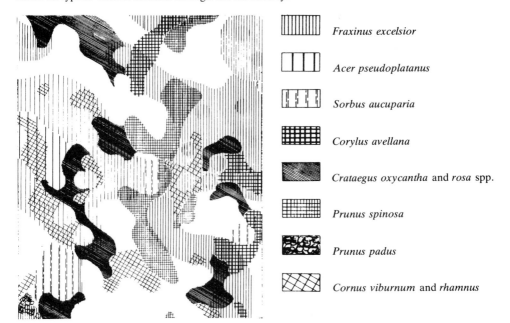

	Fraxinus excelsior
	Acer pseudoplatanus
	Sorbus aucuparia
	Corylus avellana
	Crataegus oxycantha and *rosa* spp.
	Prunus spinosa
	Prunus padus
	Cornus viburnum and *rhamnus*

83

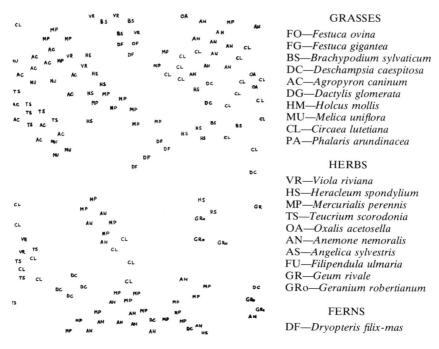

GRASSES

FO—*Festuca ovina*
FG—*Festuca gigantea*
BS—*Brachypodium sylvaticum*
DC—*Deschampsia caespitosa*
AC—*Agropyron caninum*
DG—*Dactylis glomerata*
HM—*Holcus mollis*
MU—*Melica uniflora*
CL—*Circaea lutetiana*
PA—*Phalaris arundinacea*

HERBS

VR—*Viola riviana*
HS—*Heracleum spondylium*
MP—*Mercurialis perennis*
TS—*Teucrium scorodonia*
OA—*Oxalis acetosella*
AN—*Anemone nemoralis*
AS—*Angelica sylvestris*
FU—*Filipendula ulmaria*
GR—*Geum rivale*
GRo—*Geranium robertianum*

FERNS

DF—*Dryopteris filix-mas*

Fig. 8.2 (above) The distribution of the grasses, herbs and ferns at ground level of the area of ashwood shown on Fig. 8.1.
(below) A study of the plan above indicates areas of concentration or groupings of particular species in the form of a pattern which, with the analysis in Fig. 8.1, produce design guidelines.

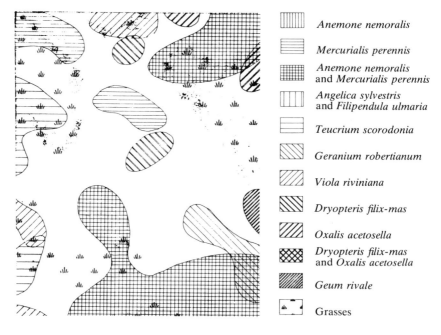

Anemone nemoralis

Mercurialis perennis

Anemone nemoralis and *Mercurialis perennis*

Angelica sylvestris and *Filipendula ulmaria*

Teucrium scorodonia

Geranium robertianum

Viola riviniana

Dryopteris filix-mas

Oxalis acetosella

Dryopteris filix-mas and *Oxalis acetosella*

Geum rivale

Grasses

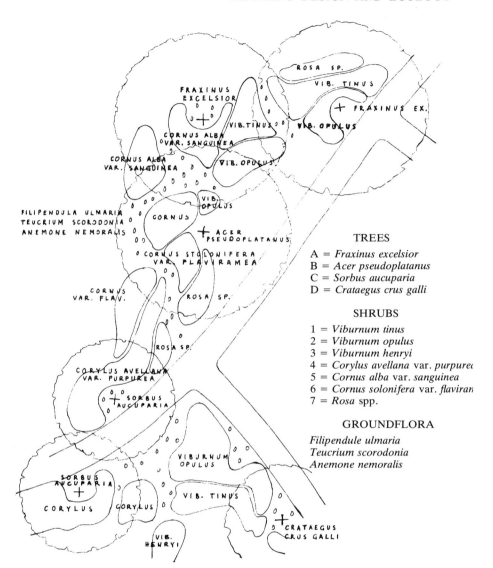

TREES

A = *Fraxinus excelsior*
B = *Acer pseudoplatanus*
C = *Sorbus aucuparia*
D = *Crataegus crus galli*

SHRUBS

1 = *Viburnum tinus*
2 = *Viburnum opulus*
3 = *Viburnum henryi*
4 = *Corylus avellana* var. *purpurea*
5 = *Cornus alba* var. *sanguinea*
6 = *Cornus solonifera* var. *flaviran*
7 = *Rosa* spp.

GROUNDFLORA

Filipendule ulmaria
Teucrium scorodonia
Anemone nemoralis

Fig. 8.3 A planting design of a part of planting designed to create sheltered spaces, and which is based upon the design guidelines shown in Figs. 8.1 and 8.2. The area covered by the plan is 60×54 m.

groundcover species would give greater emphasis to the groundcover pattern, and the spacing of the trees and shrubs could be increased to let in more light and thus allow a richer groundcover to be planted.

A realistic planting design policy, bearing in mind the difficulty of forecasting precisely what Nature will do, is to plant the whole range of species which seem the right ones on ecological grounds, but in an arrangement that accords with the landscape design brief; subsequently, the

Fig. 8.4 A planting scheme based on the native plants and the way in which they are arranged in the natural landscape.

planting is left to develop with the minimum of maintenance and the likelihood that some species will disappear and others will increase until a status quo situation is achieved. Given time and the opportunity, an experimental area set up well before planting takes place is a sensible basis for the design.

In circumstances where a 'completed' landscape is not expected quickly and where the designer will be in control of the landscape for a considerable period, or he can set up a suitable control organization, a phased planting design is a sensible approach. The aim would be to add new planting at intervals in accordance with the way in which the native vegetation might evolve from the virgin soil, for example, sowing or planting herbs or perennials which will create the cool and damp microclimate for the later planting of shrub or pioneer tree seedlings.

If the native dominant tree of an area which is naturally forest is selected as the major feature of a planting design and is planted in certain arrangements differing from the natural situation, there is a likelihood that it will thrive and create suitable niches for a range of plants more comprehensive than in the natural situation – the selection of species on this basis is discussed later (Section 8.5.).

A closer look at the arrangement of plants in the natural landscape may disclose places where the physical and climatic conditions are more favourable to the whole range of species than elsewhere: these places are often referred to as 'centres of development'; they could be given emphasis in a planting design, with the rest of the landscape restricted to something

Plate 1 Rhododendron and laburnum plants, creating a short-lived seasonal effect in a landscape predominantly evergreen.

Plate 2 An Autumn photograph of a sub-alpine grassland in Japan, with silver fir trees (*Abies mariesii*) and the grassland vegetation introducing a striking seasonal effect.

Plate 3 Flowering shrubs are often used for special effects.

Plate 4 This belt of trees has several colour variations around green, such as grey-green, yellow-green and blue-green.

Plate 5 Grey leaved plants, such as *Artemisia ludoviciana*, are an alternative in a planting scheme to the usual basic green of the vegetation.

Plate 6 White flowered plants are often more effective when planted among plants which do not flower at the same time, thus avoiding disturbance to the purity of a grey or green and white colour effect.

Plate 7 Everlasting flowers such as *Helichrysum bracteatum* often have a range of quiet colours.

Plate 8 Heather and dwarf gorse (*Ulex nanus*) add interest among the grasses to groundcover vegetation.

Plate 9 Seasonal effects from vegetation the desert in Israel are often associated v the intermittent rainfall, and are of brief duration.

10 The colour and figuration of the
of trees can add interest to a Winter
cape, as well as the tracery of the
ch system.

11 Sloping banks enable plants to be
more easily than on flat areas.

12 A marsh or bog garden, including primulas and irises among the plants happy in damp
litions.

Plate 13 Herbaceous borders which are, in this example, the main feature of the planting scheme, compared with herbaceous borders alongside wide lawns.

Plate 14 A planting scheme consisting of native plants, and which requires very little maintenance after the initial establishment period.

less than the whole range of species. Similarly, 'centres of frequency' may occur in which concentrations of a few of the species of the whole range would exist, and these could be followed in the planting design.

8.5. Plant lists

It is essential when designing planting on an ecological basis to compile a list of plant species which are native to the site, supplemented by additional species which have a relationship with them. The foundation of the list is, of course, the native plants, but often in developed countries, little remains of the natural vegetation and a reconstruction has to be made using techniques described previously, or finding areas in the region which are similar to the site in their physical characteristics, altitude and climate, and which retain the natural vegetation. The species which occur in each of these areas are likely to be most able to grow well in the site for which the planting design is to be made. Certain weed and other species growing prolifically in and around the site are also useful indicators of the habitat conditions of a site.

In compiling a list on an ecological basis which extends beyond the species native to the site, notice can be taken of the fact that many species can accept a wider range of conditions than exist in their native habitat provided competition is lacking or controlled, and this may well be the situation in a 'designed' landscape. If the list is to be useful for the various purposes required of the planting, it will in all probability be necessary to include additional species which should have an affinity with the native plants, preferably in appearance and from the same genera. Other criteria which should influence the selection are the possibility of designing planting with both close visual relationships and sharp contrasts, while the availability of plants from suppliers or other sources is a matter to be considered. 'Improved' varieties from the native species have a place in the list, as also shrub species which are not present among the native plants but have a relationship with them – a willow shrub (*Salix rosmarinifolia*) when the only native willow is the crack willow (*Salix fragilis*). The list when complete should include a wide enough range of species to emphasize visual effects and provide for various functional needs.

Two examples of typical lists are appended – one based upon a natural community in Britain and the other in the United States of America. The species included in both the natural community list and in the extended planting design list are selected to illustrate the method rather than being fully comprehensive [2].

References
[1] Wright, T. (1971), *Journal of the Institute of Landscape Architects*, No. 94, May, 12–13.
[2] Hackett, B. (1971), *Landscape Planning*, Oriel Press and Routledge & Kegan Paul, London (see Chapter 9 for a similarly based list, but compiled for landscape planning purposes).

Appendix to Chapter 8 – Plant lists

1. A natural community: Beechwood (Britain)

Trees

Fagus sylvatica
Quercus robur
Fraxinus excelsior
Prunus avium

Shrubs

Rubus fruticosus
Corylus avellana
Lonicera periclymenum
Euonymus europaeus
Rosa arvensis
Viburnum opulus

Groundflora

Oxalis acetosella
Scilla nonscripta
Galium odoratum
Fragaria vesca
Digitalis purpurea
Anemone nemorosa
Geranium robertianum
Nepeta hederacea

Plant materials for landscape design

Trees

Basic planting
Fagus crenata
Quercus rubra 'Aurea'
Fraxinus ornus
Prunus serotina

Special effects
Fagus sylvatica heterophylla
F. sylvatica purpurea
Prunus avium 'Plena'

Barriers
Crataegus monogyna
Ilex aquifolium
Fraxinus pennyslvanica

Shrubs

Basic planting
Rubus odoratus
Lonicera nitida
Euonymus latifolius
Rosa arvensis 'Splendens'

Edgings
Buxus sempervirens 'Suffruticosa'
Ligustrum japonicum
  Rotundifolium
Euonymus japonicus
  'Microphyllus'

Special effects

Rubus biflorus
Corylys avellana 'Contorta'
Euonymus yedoensis
Rosa hibernica
Viburnum carlesii

Barriers

Rosa foetida
Corylus maxima
Taxus baccata
Euonymus japonicus
Viburnum rhytidophyllum

Groundflora

Basic planting

Bromus briziformis
Ajuga reptans 'Atropurpurea'
Digitalis grandiflora
Ajuga genevensis X reptans

Perennial herbaceous

Oxalis articulata
Digitalis lutea
Anemone X hybrida 'White Queen'
Geranium pratense 'Flore Pleno'
Miscanthus sinensis
Dryopteris filix-mas

Annual herbaceous

Oxalis corniculata purpurea
Asperula azurea setosa

Bedding out

Oxalis valdiviensis
Geranium 'Renardii'
Nepeta 'Mussinii'
Pulsatilla vulgaris 'Red'

Groundcovers

Basic planting

Geranium endressii
Oxalis magellanica
Rubus caesius
Lonicera pileata

Hard wearing

Lonicera albertii
Hedera helix
Euonymus nanus

Special effects

Hedera helix var.
Rubus nutans
Geranium sanguineum
  'Prostratum'

Climbers

Rubus flagelliflorus
Lonicera periclymenum 'Serotina'
Rosa banksiae

2. A natural community: Oak-Hickory association (U.S.A.)

Trees

Quercus alba
Q. borealis maxima
Q. velutina
Ulmus americana
U. fulva
Juglans nigra
Prunus serotina
Carya cordiformis
C. ovata

Shrubs

Sambucus canadensis
Ribes cynosbati
R. missouriense
Crataegus calpodendron
C. pruinosa
C. succulenta
Malus ioensis
Viburnum prunifolium
V. rafinesquianum
Euonymus atropurpureus
Symphoricarpus orbiculatus

Groundflora

Claytonia virginica
Viola pubescens
V. papilionacea
Dentaria laciniata
Dicentra canadensis
D. cucullaria
Trillium recurvatum
Arisaema triphyllum
Polygonatum commutatum
Smilacina stellata
Podophyllum peltatum
Impatiens biflora
Eupatorium (or urticaefolium)
  rugosum

Plant materials for landscape design

Trees

Basic planting
Quercus alba
Q. borealis
Q. cerris
Juglans nigra
J. cinerea
Prunus serotina
P. virginiana
P. avium
Carya ovata
Malus baccata
Crataegus arkansana
Celtis occidentalis

Special effects
Quercus coccinea
Q. phellos
Q. robur 'Fastigiata'
Q. palustris
Juglans sieboldiana
Prunus persica 'Red leaf
P. pendula
Malus 'Strathmore'
M. 'Sundog'
M. 'Echtermeyer'
Crataegus oxycantha 'Pauli'

Barriers
Quercus robur fastigiata
Prunus hillieri spire
Malus X micromalus
M. robusta erecta
Crataegus macracantha

Shrubs

Basic planting
Sambucus canadensis maxima
Ribes aureum
R. speciosum
Malus sargentii
M. X micromalus
Viburnum acerifolium
V. trilobum
Euonymus yedoensis
Symphoricarpus chenaultii
Quercus pontica
Prunus glandulosa alboplena
P. laurocerasus 'Schipkaensis'
P. tomentosum

Special effects
Sambucus pubens
Ribes gordonianum
R. sanguineum 'Brocklebankii'
Viburnum fragrans
V. opulus 'Xanthocarpum'
V. setigerum
Euonymus alatus
(e) E. fortunei vegetus
Prunus cistens 'Henseni'
Rosa blanda

Edgings
(e) Euonymus dupont
Viburnum opulus nanum

Barriers

Ribes speciosum
Viburnum setigerum
V. wrighti
*(e) Euonymus fortunei radicans
   erecta*
(e) E. fortunei coloratus upright
(e) E. fortunei vegetas
Prunus spinosa

Groundflora

Basic planting

Pteridium latiusculum
Dryopteris spinulosa
Dryopteris thelypteris
Polystichum acrostichoides
Adiantum pedatum

Perennial/Herbaceous

Dicentra eximia
D. spectabilis
Trillium erectum
T. grandiflorum
Arisaema triphyllum
Polygonatum commutatum
Smilacina racemosa
Podophyllum peltatum
P. emodi
Aralia racemosa
Eupatorium rugosum
E. coelestinum
E. purpureum
Thalictrum polygamum
T. dioicum
! obelia cardinalis
Geranium maculatum
Mertensia virginica
Aster laevis
Hieracium villosum
Aquilegia canadensis

Annual herbaceous

Fatsia japonica (Aralia sieboldi)
Lobelia erinus compacta
Aster hy.

Bedding out

Viola spp.
Anemone spp.
Dicentra oregana
Trillium grandiflorum
Impatiens holsti hy.
I. sultani hy.

Groundcovers

**Basic planting – shade or partial
   shade conditions**

Euonymus fortunei radicans
E. fortunei 'minima'
*Symphoricarpus X chenaultii
   'Hancock'*
Hypericum moserianum

Hard wearing

Hedera helix
Vinca minor
Poa compressa
Agrostis alba
Festuca elatior

Special effects

Eonymus fortunei coloratus

Climbers

Aristolochia durior
Celastrus scandens
C. virginiana
Lonicera japonica 'Halliana'
Lycium chinense
Polygonum auberti
Parthenocissus quinquefolia

CHAPTER 9

Seasonal effects

The appearance of vegetation at different times of the year remains constant to a considerable degree in areas with the two extremes of climate – the humid tropical and the sub-arctic – this being due in the former to the evergreen vegetation with the only seasonal changes coming from the flowers, which are small in area compared with the leaf cover. In the arid tropical and the alpine flora parts of the world there occur impressive, but short-lived seasonal effects associated with occasional rain in the former (Plate 9) and the late Spring of the latter. In the temperate parts of the world, with deciduous forests in the lowlands and coniferous forests in the uplands, the change in the lowlands from a leaf cover to bare branches every late Autumn is, in itself, a striking seasonal effect.

9.1. Winter appearance

There are numerous books and catalogues of plants which discuss and list plants which will give effects like 'spring flowering', 'autumn leaf colour' and 'colourful berries'; a selection of these books and catalogues is a necessary part of the equipment of a designer in landscape, and it is not proposed to describe in this Chapter effects given by different plants, but to describe only the types of planting which form the basis of seasonal effects. The Winter season in the temperate climates has a smaller range of visual interest from plants than the other three seasons. The colour and tracery of the branches of some species is a valuable addition to the effects created by evergreen vegetation and colourful berries, and these latter are unlikely to survive through the whole winter (Plate 10). A familiar example is the red stemmed dogwood (*Cornus alba 'Sibirica'*) which can highlight a Winter landscape, and with increased effect when used in association with white stemmed birch (*Betula pendula*) or with evergreen vegetation. The Himalayan Birch (*Betula utilis*) with its red brown branches creates visual interest in a landscape when associated with the dark evergreen vegetation of some hollies and conifers.

The branch system of some trees, and to a lesser extent some shrub species, gives visual interest in the Winter, and is a neglected area in planting

92

design. In the discussion on the habit of plants (Section 4.1), attention was drawn to this interest, and in order to provide for it, the plants selected should be planted so that they will be seen as they mature against the sky or some other uncomplicated background (see Fig. 6.8); this will involve skill in the design so that the effect is viewed from several positions, except when fastigiate species are planted thickly so that a fence-like appearance is created and the viewing positions are limited. The ancient practice of coppicing suitable species like alder and hazel (*Corylus avellana*) also produces this effect. Another visual effect can be provided by trees planted equidistant on a grid and spaced so that the crowns just meet when mature; if the ground is clear, the observer can enjoy looking up at the tracery of the branches as they form a 'vaulted ceiling' to the landscape.

In some temperate parts of the world, such as parts of the U.S.A., the grass groundcover appears to die above ground in Winter, compared with other temperate parts where the grass remains green. In the eyes of some observers the change of colour from the Summer green to a pale yellow/brown is interesting. But to other observers, the change is an uninteresting off-season effect which to some extent can be avoided by arranging the grass areas as part of a pattern, the other elements being formed by bare soil and evergreen groundcover plants.

9.2. Seasonal change

Although the aim of some people is to have a planting scheme with a sequence of colour – at least from early Spring to late Autumn – this is not typical of the natural landscape in which the colourful periods usually come in short 'bursts'. It can also be argued that a continuous sequence of colour will lose its impact compared with 'bursts' of colour separated by quiet intervals (Fig. 9.1). If, however, the aim is a continuous sequence of colour, a good solution is to arrange for groups of plants selected for their different flowering times to be located in different parts of the landscape so that variety in interest does not occur in the same places at the same time.

The idea of 'bursts' of colour can be made even more effective by selecting only those plants within the range of colours associated with the seasons. Thus, plants with yellow and blue flowers for the Spring; deep blue, white and pink for early Summer; scarlet, deep yellow and purple in late Summer; brown and purple from leaves and flowers in the Autumn; deep green and brown leaves with scarlet berries in Winter.

9.3. Seasonal effects and landscape structure

A common difficulty met in planting design for seasonal effect is that many plants with effective colour from their flowers lack interest if they are judged from the point of view of plants which contribute to the structure of the landscape. For example, the poor appearance of a hybrid tea rose, apart from its flowers, has already been mentioned (see Section 7.6); the lilac (*Syringa* spp.) is another example, being a plant with a beautiful display of

Fig. 9.1 Wild cherry trees introduce a sudden and brief change to the appearance of the edge of a mixed woodland.

flowers, but mundane in its leaves and branch system. The solution to this problem lies in the emphasis which can be given to the frame within which the plants are located; a frame of strong visual effect can reduce the impact of the appearance of plants with a poor leaf and branch system upon the observer. In the example of the lilac, planting a low and dense shrub border or constructing a low wall in front will help to hide some of the untidy effect. Alternatively, because lilacs are large shrubs, they can be used as a background to other plants giving seasonal interest at times when the lilacs are not in flower.

There is a popular demand for small trees with conspicuous flowers, such as cherries and almonds. During the long period when these trees are not flowering, they should be considered in a planting design either in association with small scale intimate landscapes, i.e. within the confines of a well-enclosed garden, or mingled in among other trees and shrubs of various heights so that they have a place in the idea referred to previously of 'bursts' of colour occurring in different places at different times. In Britain, the native wild cherries (*Prunus padus* and *Prunus avium*) and some of the crab apples (*Malus* spp.) have the freer form and habit which enables them to be less conspicuous and harmonize better in the non-flowering period with other plants. It is important that plants selected for their seasonal effect should be useful in planting design at other times of the year; for example, the formal habit of the branch system of many of the so-called flowering cherries might form the basis of a Winter appearance in the manner described previously.

9.4. Bedding-out and annual plants

The way in which bedding-out plants have been used during the last century has brought unfavourable comment in landscape design circles, apart from the fact that it is an expensive practice. Nevertheless, bedding-out plants give seasonal variety, and there are places in a landscape where their use can be appropriate if the design of the planting is more sensitive and less artificial than the elaborate patterns, clock faces and coats of arms, or the lines of 'one *pelargonium* and one *lobelia*'. A more sensitive result will come from selecting plants with colours sympathetic to the range of colours of the local or regional landscape, and arranging them in a pattern based upon the natural groundflora patterns, such as in a woodland or heathland.

The time of year which in many parts of the world is lacking in plants with visual impact is late Summer. It is not by any means a disaster to have a quiet period in the appearance of landscape, but this late Summer period can be given interest by sowing annuals which flower at this time, or a little later than their normal time through late sowing. Annuals have lost some of their popularity, possibly because of the work involved in these days when the objective is a 'no maintenance' landscape. In common with the herbaceous border, annuals can also give seasonal effects as well as their particular contribution in late Summer.

9.5. Autumn colour

Autumn colours produced by the leaves of trees and shrubs in temperate parts of the world are a welcome change to the landscape before Winter sets in. In order to produce the greatest visual interest, however, plants with this seasonal effect should be associated with evergreen or coniferous species, or with deciduous species with a late leaf fall, in order that the warm Autumn colours are highlighted against the cooler greens. Similarly, deciduous species with prominent berries, like *Rosa moyesii* or *Cotoneaster bullatus*, are less effective in late Autumn and early Winter unless seen against a background of evergreen plants. Both deciduous and evergreen species which are planted for their berrying effect should be planted in quantity in order to make the necessary visual impact, although one plant in a small garden can suffice.

CHAPTER 10

Planting design and the habitat

The most successful results from the ecological and appearance points of view in the planting of a landscape are likely to occur when the concept of the site being a habitat or comprising several habitats is uppermost in the design policy. Some sites may already have clearly defined habitats, while other sites may have features which can be strengthened to bring about the physical basis of a habitat; the planting can then be designed to accord with the various conditions. For example, a bank gently sloping towards the midday sun, and which does not suffer from soil infertility or excessive soil drainage, constitutes a favourable habitat for perennials, compared with planting a herbaceous border in an open flat landscape. Also, a low-lying and badly drained wet area can form a favourable habitat for a 'bog garden', especially with some control of the soil moisture.

The various techniques for modifying the physical conditions of habitats are explained in the numerous books on horticultural and arboricultural practices, on soils and on drainage. With these techniques, heavy soils can be made light and vice versa. Soil moisture, for example, can be retained by mulching or by creating shade from the planting of large plants among the smaller ones, or by diverting run-off towards the habitat. Acid and alkaline soils can be modified one way or another by the addition of lime or peat. Concerning soil fertility, information is readily available on how to achieve this, but the designer is faced with the problem whether to use artificial chemical fertilizers or the natural fertilizers of manure or the compost heap; apart from the cost of modifying soil types, it is preferable to design the planting to fit the soil, rather than vice-versa. Shelter and the correct illumination from the sun or sky are other factors to be evaluated in analysing a landscape as a habitat or a series of them. The aim in this Chapter is to suggest that various types of physical condition in the landscape, resulting from, for example, topography and orientation, are best regarded in planting design as habitats in the ecological sense, rather than merely as areas given to particular visual results. The examples chosen take into account both 'natural habitats' and those likely to be created in some landscape designs.

10.1. Grassland planting

It is not proposed that maintained grass lawns should be discussed because these are special groundcover areas, usually located for some functional or aesthetic purpose. Our interest is the natural grassland habitat as a particular kind of vegetational complex existing mainly as prairie, savannah or veldt landscapes, and possibly in parts of some upland areas. The three characteristic types of vegetation which should be considered in a planting design based upon the grassland habitat are those grass species which produce prominent flower heads; perennials which can compete with the grasses and preferably do not flower at the same time; and dispersed shrubs so arranged as to give some shelter from winds, but leaving adequate areas of grassland for views across the landscape. Access through this type of planting for functional and visual pleasure can be provided by mown grass paths (Fig. 10.1) or the more expensive raised decking.

The example in the wild which is closest to the vegetation of a grassland habitat in Britain is the country road verge. When this is left unmown and undisturbed by weedkillers its appearance in Spring and Summer is enriched by wildflowers, such as Bloody Crane's Bill (*Geranium sanguineum*), knapweed (*Centaurea nigra*) and yarrow (*Achillea millefolium*), and in the late Summer and often well into Winter by the dead flower heads of wild grasses, such as loose silky-bent (*Agrostis spica-venti*) and black twitch (*Alopecurus myosuroides*).

Fig. 10.1 The mown grass path enables the flora of the grassland to be observed without damage.

The main problem in designing the planting and sowing for the grassland habitat is predicting its future. For example, some of the useful plants are annuals and may not find they can survive from their seed; also the element of competition is a major factor because of the difficulty of controlling dominating plants among the grasses. Restricting soil fertility by mechanical devices, such as mixing sub-soil with the topsoil can reduce competition; even so, maintenance by thinning and cutting back dominating plants and their root systems is likely to be essential for 3 or 4 years after planting and sowing. In the Shenandoah National Park in the U.S.A., a small area is kept as pasture under a management régime of controlled grazing in order to preserve an example of the agricultural landscape of the region before the farmers moved to the newly opened-up and profitable Mid-West; if this management régime was not operated, the land would return to natural forest, as elsewhere in the park. Similarly, controlled grazing and other experimental techniques are being used to prevent the 'invasion' of birch trees in the heather/grassland/juniper landscape of the Lüneberg Heide Nature Park in West Germany. Management of upland pasture by burning is another example (see also Section 14.1).

Experimentation will disclose what plants can exist side by side without invading each other's territory. The aim of the planting plan should be, however, to achieve an undulating effect in the height of the plants, falling to an even low height against footpaths. While a designer will often try to achieve contrast between grass and herb species, the advantage of interplanting vigorous grass species among the herbs is that the latter are kept in an upright position and are thus more effective; for this purpose, tough grasses like crested dogstail (*Cynosurus cristatus*) are typical examples, while the fescues with their delicate flower heads are better grown in groups by themselves and surrounded by other plants with substantial leaves against which the filigree pattern can be seen. The arrangement of the herb species should comprise both concentrated groups of one species and groups of different mixed species. Shrub planting is acceptable in small groups, but the species selected should not have prominent visual characteristics, which would compete with the grassland plants, except when junipers, for example, on downlands or heathlands are intended to be the most important visual element (see Fig. 2.4).

A special kind of grassland planting is the use of tufted grasses, like *Festuca glauca*, as a monocultural groundcover; this has been used frequently in the U.S.A. as a component of a pattern of plants, and in West Berlin as a complete groundcover on the sandy soil (Fig. 10.1).

10.2. Sloping banks

Sloping banks (Plate 11) have the advantage of enabling the planting on them to be more easily seen than planting on a flat surface. Considered as a habitat, the exposure to, or protection from, damaging winds, and the fertility status have a marked effect upon the vegetation. When soil fertility

Fig. 10.2 The tufted grass – *Festuca glauca* – makes an unusual and effective grassland landscape in the sandy soil of West Berlin.

is low and drainage excessive, as with some roadside cuttings, plants like gorse and broom among a limited range will often grow readily, but when the soil is of good average fertility, a habitat is provided for a wide range of plants.

Perhaps to differentiate the fertile sloping bank from the herbaceous border, the planting should mix both shrubs and perennials. It is also a habitat in which the smaller of the 'species' roses seem to exist happily and look right for the situation – examples are *Rosa macrantha* and *Rosa pimpinellifolia lutea*, which benefit as small plants from their crowns being seen more easily than at an angle from eye level when planted on level ground. Perennial plants which have substantial leaves, giving an appearance of strength, help to overcome any visual impression that the bank might be unstable and subject to erosion.

Fig. 10.3 A woodland on a slope in Japan with a low moss groundcover enables the tree trunks to create an interesting landscape.

Trees can be planted on sloping banks with good effect, although the size of trees suggests a long slope. If the trunks are free from lateral branches for a considerable height above ground, and the groundflora is low, the view of the tree trunks 'ascending' the slope is effective (Fig. 10.3), particularly with beech trees; but the limited groundflora associated with beech woodlands can lead to erosion in these circumstances. Ivy is a useful plant on slopes in association with trees.

An objective in planting infertile sloping banks is likely to be the prevention of erosion, and for this purpose a close cover is essential. If the slope has an acid sandy soil, it is likely in temperate climates that heather species will colonize, interspersed with grasses like wavy hair grass (*Deschampsia flexuosa*) and browntop grass (*Agrostis tenuis*). Gorse and its dwarf form are also plants suited to this habitat.

Plants with long trailing stems are effective on slopes, common examples being *Rosa wichuriana* and the bramble (*Rubus spectabilis*). Also, when the slope does not receive a great deal of direct light, and the soil is suitable, azaleas are well displayed in these circumstances.

10.3. Woodland fringe

The transition in a natural situation from the shrubs and groundcover plants of a woodland to the open landscape (Fig. 10.4) does not take place suddenly, but rather by some modification to the vegetation as a result of the improving illumination, the increased exposure, and the lessening drip from

Fig. 10.4 The edge to the woodland has trees and shrubs of a smaller size and different character from the woodland behind.

the trees as their density decreases. These habitat modifications made possible the introduction of the woodland garden of the later half of the 19th century, when plants like lilies (*Lilium* spp.), lily of the valley (*Convallaria majalis*) and sweet woodruff (*Galium odoratum*) were introduced among the cleared undergrowth at the edge of a path system through and along the edge of woodland; other commonly used plants were primulas and ferns. The objective should be, however, to avoid the appearance of a separate planting scheme, and the idea of a gradual transition, even in a small space, is more suitable.

The increased illumination, compared with inside the woodland, suggests that some trees and shrubs with conspicuous flowers are proper for the habitat. Nevertheless, species which have a visual or generic connection with woodland plants are preferable to plants fully at home in the open landscape. The native cherries in Britain are examples of suitable edge of woodland trees, and the use of an occasional prominent hybrid like the purple beech (*Fagus sylvatica 'Riversii'*) or the deciduous European larch (*Larix decidua*) at the edge of a coniferous woodland adds interest and a sense of transition from a closed to an open landscape at the boundary.

Sometimes, the aim in a landscape design will be to have a distinct and dense boundary between woodland and the open landscape, such as is formed by planting evergreens between the trees like Portugal laurel (*Prunus lusitanica*) or rhododendron species. Sometimes, the distinct and dense boundary can be kept back a few metres into the woodland so that the trees and a low groundcover soften the appearance of the boundary.

A sensitive planting of the woodland fringe can be achieved by bringing out suitable shrub species of the woodland beyond the trees which can accept the increased illumination and adding some sun-loving shrub species. Large boulders may be used along the fringe and into the woodland interplanted with small edge-of-woodland plants to provide a physical boundary, with special interest at close quarters from the small plants in the sheltered niches formed by the boulders.

The woodland fringe can be looked at in the reverse way as the edge of adjoining grassland, with shade tolerant grass species penetrating a few metres into the woodland without any shrub cover. Grasslands belong to open landscapes in general, but a few species are tolerant of shade, such as the hard fescue (*Festuca longifolia* var. *'Biljart'*), rough stalked meadow grass (*Poa trivialis*) and wood meadow grass (*Poa nemoralis*).

10.4. Marsh or bog garden

There has always been a tendency to underrate the quality of marshlands as a landscape type, possibly because of their lack of variety in vegetation and topography. The small wet areas, however, draining the immediate surroundings, form contrasting habitats and are capable of considerable planting interest. Many of the plants favouring high water table conditions fall into two distinct categories regarding appearance – those with thin sword-like leaves and those having large broad leaves. Contrast is also associated with the height of many plants in marshy areas – low grasses and plants like the marsh marigold (*Calthea palustris*) growing near to the tall yellow flag (*Iris pseudacorus*). If trees or shrubs are growing around parts of the perimeter of a marsh or bog area, the varying conditions of illumination will add to the range of plants suited to high water table conditions.

In designing the planting of a marsh or bog garden (Plate 12), the height of the plants in relation to the line of sight needs careful consideration, because access among the plants is likely to be limited to viewing from the periphery or from a path system raised above the water table. Thus, in general, plants low in height should occupy the foreground, although the occasional group of tall plants in that position helps to give unity to the planting scheme and prevents all the planting being seen in one view. It is appropriate to arrange larger groups of a species than is usual in a herbaceous border – an arrangement in keeping with the large areas of a species in natural marshlands.

The range of plants available includes the water loving species of 'sword-like' plants (some irises, sedges, rushes, and some bamboos), low growing plants with conspicuous flowers (marsh marigolds, globe flowers, and candelabra primulas), tall plants with conspicuous flowers (*Astilbes, Lythrum*, and day lilies), fern species, and the large leaved plants (*Gunnera, Rodgersia*, and *Ligularia*). Shrubs favouring marsh or bog habitat conditions are the red-stemmed dogwood and shrub willows. With such a wide range of plants, the planting design of a marsh or bog garden can produce a rich landscape in itself, compared with other garden elements like the herbaceous border or a parterre.

Winter appearance is a problem with a marsh or bog garden because the high water table is not helpful in trying to achieve a neat soil surface when the vegetation has died. Some of the sedges, rushes and bamboos will remain in evidence for most of the Winter, although losing their green colour. Evergreen ferns such as hart's tongue fern (*Phyllitis scolopendrium*) or shrubs with Winter interest like the red-stemmed dogwood will help to maintain interest if arranged as a pattern standing out from the decaying vegetation.

Interest can be given to the planting by minor variations in the ground level, producing varying differences between the soil surface and the water table, thus widening the range of suitable plants. The designer may also wish to make some minor changes in the surrounding ground levels so that at the perimeter the change in plant species can be sudden or gradual from the high water table plants to those suited to normal water table conditions. A more complicated change can be arranged by a bank with normal water table planting and a further low lying area with the water table at a depth between that of the wet area and the normal depth, and planted with species suited to the 'transition' conditions.

10.5. Waterside and aquatic planting

The conditions associated with marsh or bog gardens are not dissimilar to those of waterside habitats (Fig. 10.5), but there are likely to be greater variations in the level of the water and hence in the water table of the banks; the flow of the current in streamside habitats also influences plant life. A major difference, however, that should influence the designer is the visual unity of the adjoining water surface, and he or she may wish to reflect this unity in the planting design, or alternatively consider whether the result would be monotonous. In natural waterside landscapes, changes in species result from changes in the soil, in the steepness of the bank and in the flow of the stream; these changes do not usually occur frequently if a stream is followed through the countryside. Uses of the water, such as boating and fishing, require access and this will affect the planting in some places.

Waterside planting also involves the control of erosion; in this respect, the to and fro movement of wave action on the shores of a pond or lake can be more of a problem disturbing planting than the continuous flow in one direction of a stream because of the loosening of the root systems. A grass cover is the simplest form of waterside vegetation, both in the number of suitable species and in appearance; but it can hold its own against a current flowing at about 2.3 m/s and is not so severely affected by wave action as taller plants. Grass species which are tolerant of waterside conditions are *Phleum pratense*, *Festuca rubra* and *Agrostis alba* var. *stolonifera*.

Reeds, rushes and tall grasses like *Glyceria maxima* and *Phalaris arundinaceae* are suitable for a current flowing at 1.5 m/s, but *Glyceria* is not

Fig. 10.5 Typical waterside vegetation in a natural situation.

happy in wave action zones. Special planting techniques are usually necessary to overcome damage during the initial growth period, for example, planting in small ditches above the wave impact, or structural devices like temporary low dykes or fascine matting. A fringe of willow or alder species is likely to stand up to a stream flow of 3.5 m/s and is a very natural kind of planting along watersides, but it does restrict access and vision. Among the willows, *Salix aurita* and *S. purpurea* var. *uralensis* are suitable species, while *S. fragilis* hybrids can survive alternating periods of shallow water cover and draw down (Fig. 10.6).

When an observer looks across water to an opposite bank which is further away than about 10 m, the surface of the water forms a bright foreground, often with some sky reflection. As a result, the planting of waterside plants may lose some of its effect unless there is a dark background which could be achieved with dense planting of trees and shrubs, with indentations to form shadow and shade effects. This suggestion also adds to the interest of the reflection of the planting in the water.

Microclimatic effects have to be taken into account in planting around the exposed areas in the landscape resulting from ponds and lakes, not only from winds, but also from the reflective capability of water in extending the effects of light or warmth when the angle of reflection of the sun becomes lower to meet the waterside plants. East and West orientations when the sun is low in the sky should influence minor changes in the planting.

Planting into submerged soil can be effected with three types of plants –

Fig. 10.6 Shrub willows at the water's edge.

the emergent plants with stems and leaves rising out of the water like the flowering rush (*Butomus umbellatus*), the surface plants like water lilies (*Nymphae* spp.), and the submerged plants like sago pondweed (*Potamogeton pectinatus*). All of these types are important for a healthy state of balance between fish, insects and plants which is important to maintain because some aquatic plants seem able to take over the habitat more easily than land-loving plants.

The design of aquatic planting is logically a reflection of the depths of the water, modified by the current in streams and by waves in ponds and lakes. A basic decision is the proportion of vegetation seen on the surface compared with the unvegetated surface area of water; this decision is particularly important with small pools, and means a decision whether the planting or the water is more important in the design of the landscape. Within the planted areas interest can be created by fragile plants in the sheltered niches formed by groups of bulrushes (*Scirpus lacustris*).

10.6. Planting and hard materials

Designers have often found that planting contained by walling or paving opened up many visual possibilities, particularly in the contrast between

Fig. 10.7 An example of planting in association with paving and sculptural elements.

uniform surfaces of the hard materials and the varying colour and textural effects of the plants (Fig. 10.7). In paved areas, planting can take place in pockets left in the paving or in wide joints.

When pockets are left in stone flag or brick paving, it is preferable to use plants with a strong and definite form or habit; plants with a fine overall texture (unless their colour makes a strong impact) merely disturb the even quality of the paving, instead of providing an intended contrast. Plants like irises with their sword-like leaves, or *Bergenia cordifolia* with their large rounded leaves and flowering 'spires' have this strong character. The reverse situation, however, is appropriate when provision is made for planting in wide joints left in the paving; in these circumstances, plants with a moss-like texture are suitable because they maintain the pattern of the jointing and do not compete with the paving – examples are the sandwort (*Arenaria balearica*) and *Cotula squalida*.

Paths and paved areas are frequently bordered with planting which can have many varied species because of the uniformity of the hard materials. If the adjacent area is planted with a single groundcover species for a considerable length, there are grounds on the score of appearance for avoiding an uninterrupted straight line between the planting and the paving, for example, by allowing the groundcover plants to grow irregularly over the edge of the paving, or by arranging a 'broken' edge to the paving.

Walling in association with planting occurs with plant boxes or raised beds (Fig. 10.8), with a change in level, and with climbing plants; also an interesting effect results when plants droop over walling. The colour and

Fig. 10.8 Planting in raised beds – an alternative to this formal planting is based upon the arrangement of plants in a natural situation.

scale of the texture of walling (i.e. the size of the bricks or stones, and the nature of concrete or rendered surfaces) are matters for consideration in planting decisions; in this respect, the colours of bricks present more problems than with stones. A dark red brick accepts the colour of dark evergreen or grey-leaved climbing plants, and a dark blue brick is an effective background for climbers with white or yellow flowers and with bright green leaves. Pink and blue flowers raise colour relationship anomalies if associated with many of the red brick colours, and texture relationships are not very successful when plants with very large leaves are growing against a brick wall.

Planting in association with stonework in the kind of rock garden usually constructed is rarely seen as an expression of the natural landscape of the site, which is more likely to be forest or grassland. The designer will have to decide whether the planting is better designed within a terrace system according with the design of a building on the site or with an abstract design; on the other hand, the aim may be to simulate planting and hard material associations met in natural landscape, such as in a scree. In the case of a terrace system, it is appropriate to select plants for their visual interest and relationship, whereas with simulated rock outcrops or screes, plants which are low and spreading are typical of these habitats in the wild (see Fig. 6.4). With the simulated scree, tufted grasses form a sensitive contrast to the low and spreading plants. There is a tendency for this kind of habitat to have its devotees of the plants rather than of the overall effect, with the result that

107

small areas are accorded to the many intriguing plants. Large areas of one species contrasting with small areas of other species produces a better visual result and closer to a natural situation.

If the plants in a rock garden are selected on the basis of a particular natural association of plants, the flowering season is likely to be limited, and the designer may feel justified in extending the plant list. The most familiar example of rock garden planting which reflects the appearance of a particular association in the natural landscape is the use of various heathers (*Erica* and *Calluna* spp.), and these can be selected to produce a sequence of colour throughout the year.

10.7. The border

Planting alongside a lawn or paving (Plate 13) is a familiar element in a landscape design, and it has been the practice to use it as a place for a wide range of plants, instead of a place for related plants, such as a collection of *Rosa* species. Many of the principles applicable to planting in borders have been stated in previous Chapters on the visual characteristics and relationships of plants. Some further comment will not be out of place. With regard to colour effects, unless the objective is a gradual modulation through most colours, the warm colours are better used as a single colour with varying depths and moving not too far from the central colour; for instance, reds with variations towards orange and purple, and tints of these colours down to cream. Plants with blue flowers are, however, more effective if the colour is intense and if contrasted with yellow flowers. Plants with white and blue flowers in a section of a border are favoured, although care is needed in siting the plants with white flowers in order that they do not break up the appearance of the border.

The planting of a border which has a hedge or wall background along one side requires a different approach compared with a border seen from both sides. One side of the former kind is sheltered, while visibility is a feature of both sides of the latter kind. The orientation of a herbaceous or annual border of the former kind is best towards the South-West because the flowers and leaves after a Spring frost can gently thaw before the sun comes round. A technical matter in the design of the one-sided border is the necessity of leaving a bare strip between the planting and the background for access.

There are no strict rules regarding the width of a border, but if it is less than 1.5 m, it is preferable to treat it as a uniform strip, especially if it has a uniform background, which would indicate groundcover plants. A width of 5.5 m is perhaps as far as an observer is able to see the whole of the planting, assuming the plants rise in height from near the observer. A width of 11.0 m, on this basis, would be the maximum for the border seen from each side. Width in relation to plant visibiiity is not the only criterion, because the width needs consideration in relation to the length. Also, the larger the border, especially in width, the greater should be the number of plants in any one group of a single species or variety, and this will be influenced by the size of the plants. As a rough guide, a narrow border about 15 m long might have in groups 10 species of small plants and 3 species of large plants, the number of species increasing up to 20 and 12 respectively for a wide border about 25 m long. The designer should also take into account the possibility of a few of the tall plants grouped as a 'spire' or 'spires', instead of as a mass effect. In a narrow border up to 2.0 m wide, plants taller than 1.5 m will appear out of scale.

There are many ways of massing the various species in a border. A gradual increase in height from the front to the rear, or middle, while relying upon the colour of the flowers to produce interest, is one approach, and a hill and valley effect created by plants of various heights is another. The planting of occasional clumps of tall plants along the observing edge adds interest because it will prevent all the planting being visible all the time. Generally, shrub borders are designed with less attention to the 'contouring' of the top of the vegetation, because they are used more as a background or structural element of the landscape.

The planting of a herbaceous border should also take into account the effect of the decaying foliage of the earliest plants to flower. Thus, late flowering plants should be planted as far as possible in front of the early flowering plants. When bulbs are included in the planting scheme, they can be placed so that the decaying foliage is obscured by perennials developing at a later date.

Herbaceous borders at the edge of grass lawns usually have straight or wavy line boundaries which in practice can be softened by selecting plants for the edges and, as they develop, overlap the edges. A wavy line accentuates the effect, but the designer should beware of too much curvature on plan, which often appears too sharp when seen by an observer. Shrubs, of course, soften the edge to a greater extent than herbaceous plants.

10.8. Contact with plants

The interest in educational circles in bringing the pupil into the landscape, instead of bringing plants into the classroom, is all part of a movement to have closer contact between people and vegetation, including also other living creatures in the landscape (Fig. 10.9). Herbaceous borders, rock gardens and other elements of designed landscapes are for visual enjoyment from outside, instead of bringing the observer into a close physical relationship with the plants, so that he or she becomes a participant in the living landscape. For this reason alone, the idea of conceiving areas in the landscape as habitats and approaching the design of the planting on this thesis is sensible. A planting design which is based upon the idea of a woodland into which spaces are cut or left for people to occupy and enjoy is a simple example of close contact between people and vegetation.

When the observer is underneath a tree canopy, he or she experiences a close physical relationship with vegetation because of the control exercised

Fig. 10.9 A planting scheme in a Dutch housing area, based upon a natural situation, and which encourages contact with the plants by the residents (courtesy of Ian C. Laurie).

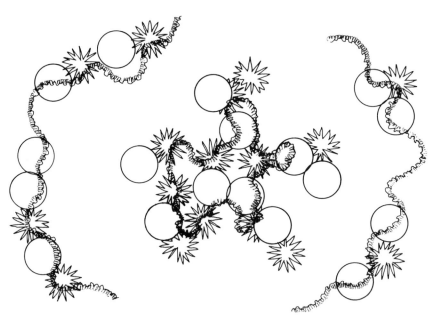

Fig. 10.10 A planting scheme which provides several microclimates as the position of the sun and the direction of the wind change.

by the canopy over the plants and animals in the habitat below. The problem with this kind of planting design is the lack of illumination, particularly direct sunlight. A solution is to have trees grouped in the centre, with spaces around. As a result, variations in sunlight, shade and shelter from the wind are found in the spaces at different times of the day; the observer can remain under the canopy at its edge whilst enjoying sunshine (Fig. 10.10).

Planting which is based upon a natural community of plants and is purposely neglected brings the observer closer to Nature than a conventional planting design, provided access is possible. If a 'neglected' area is small, the impression of neglect and untidiness is strong. But if the area is large, the so-called neglect and untidiness of a natural plant community is acceptable. In a small area this difficulty can be overcome by outlining the planting at the boundary of the use or viewing areas with a narrow strip of mown grass, or by large boulders, both giving an impression of containing a wild area (Fig. 10.11).

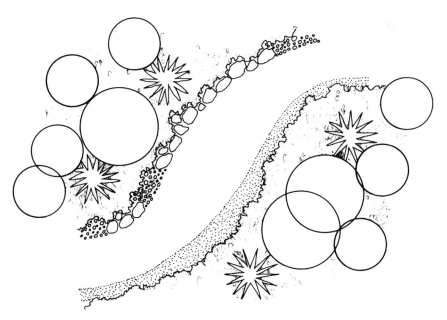

Fig. 10.11 Two solutions to the problem of wild planting in a small area and the consequent fear of an untidy appearance. Boulders are used on one side of the path with the planting growing between them. On the other side, a mown grass edge gives a neat effect.

111

CHAPTER 11

Planting design in practice

The question may well be asked whether the principles which should be taken into account in planting design are different or selected when applied in practice to urban, compared with rural, areas. For example, the influence of the natural landscape of a site is not so obvious in urban areas, although this might be considered to be the reason for the planting design recouping some of the elements of the natural landscape. Also, some agreement between the plants selected for both urban and rural areas makes a small contribution to strengthening the ties between town and country within a region. If, however, we take into account the planting tradition of a country, it is acceptable if a small number of exotic species from other countries is included in urban landscapes, and a small number of species native to other regions of the country in question is included in rural landscapes. With regard to the remaining proportion of the planting in both urban and rural areas, this could be limited to the native vegetation of the present climatic era; alternatively, many trees and shrubs, introduced perhaps more than 200 years ago, have become part of the traditional landscape, especially if they grow well, and more especially if they regenerate naturally. Unless the planting policy is based entirely on the native plant community, the principle outlined for urban and rural areas is an acceptable compromise between purely native species and exotics, and does not rule out the attainment of a satisfactory grouping of plant species from the ecological point of view.

11.1. Commercial woodlands and forests

The economic situation often acts against the possibility of using only native species of tree for large areas of commercial forestry. But commercial forestry is unlikely to become bankrupt if the tree species is changed to accord with the natural vegetation boundaries; this concession in itself would produce a small but welcome change to the monotony of commercial forestry, and this can be still further relieved by planting the small areas unsuitable for producing commercial timber with trees suited to these areas (Fig. 11.1), as in a narrow indented valley with exposed rocks and small, badly drained areas. While the earlier policy of planting a narrow margin of

Fig. 11.1 An example of a natural forest in Switzerland with some variation in the species, and which is managed on a commercial basis.

exotic trees around a planted coniferous forest in some countries was well intentioned, the result had little sympathy with the landscape. A better result is to introduce deciduous and evergreen tree species into the first 20 m of a coniferous forest (Fig. 11.2), gradually reducing the number of deciduous trees until there remain only the conifers. In Britain, some deciduous and evergreen species were used traditionally as nurse trees, such as hawthorn, birch and holly[1].

Forests with mixed deciduous and coniferous species are visually acceptable in many landscapes, but the Winter appearance needs to be considered because a mixture like the alternation of one conifer with one deciduous tree in that season is monotonous. It is preferable to vary this type of planting with areas planted entirely with deciduous or coniferous trees, and with the boundaries following natural boundaries and the topography, and thus meeting to some extent the foresters' problem of extracting mixed species. The deciduous larch among other conifers produces similar problems, especially in the Winter appearance (Fig. 11.3).

The objective of the maximum return from commercial forests is usually less strict in the case of the yield from smaller woodlands which have a tradition of serving various purposes, except that the current interest in commercial forests as recreational assets with a financial return can reduce the emphasis on the marketable timber aspect. If the objective in the planting of small woodlands is primarily the support of a game and wildlife population, several different kinds of niches should be created so that there

Fig. 11.2 A coniferous forest edge of deciduous species.

Fig. 11.3 The Winter appearance of the larch tree – a deciduous conifer – can cause visual problems in a coniferous forest unless the boundaries of the different species are arranged with regard to natural boundaries and visual considerations. In this example the two kinds of tree are visually integrated.

114

are fully protected places using broad-leaved evergreen shrubs like Portugal laurel or berrying shrubs like wild roses. Some conifer trees will provide Winter shelter, while deciduous trees of different heights for nesting and spaced at varied intervals will also give different degrees of illumination on the ground and thus encourage various groundflora – the aim being to provide a rich flora. It is important to leave spaces in the tree planting as small glades and to plant them with species like snowberry or common laurel in order to produce a rich crop of berries; some of the spaces should be arranged to give clear outlets for the flight of game birds[2].

Some woodlands are designed specifically for shelter purposes with quick-growing and wind-resistant species which do not always accord with the local landscape, but the designer who does take it into account has to decide whether species selected entirely for shelter are acceptable or whether some compromise is possible, either through a mixture of species or acceptance of a slower rate of growth. Apart from this dilemma of species selection, the shape and manner in which shelter belts relate to the topography (Fig. 11.4) are also important to the degree of shelter, and with regard to the local landscape (see Section 13.3). However, these latter decisions are made at the landscape planning and agricultural practice levels.

The management technique of coppicing, as applied to woodlands, is rarely used today, compared with the vast areas of new afforestation. It can produce a particular visual result from a thicket of tall stems of comparatively small diameter, and can be very useful for local screening

Fig. 11.4 Shelter planting in an open landscape which is well related to the topography.

purposes, but the cutting has to be carried out on a phased cycle to avoid temporary loss of the screen. If the coppiced woodland is to be accepted today for visual or screening purposes, it will in most cases need to have a commercial value in the particular kind of timber produced. Trees which have had this value and respond to the coppicing method of management are willows, alder, birch and sweet chestnut (*Castanea sativa*).

At the time when so many woodlands, belts and groups of trees were planted in the countryside in Britain in the later 17th to early 19th centuries, the species selected were generally from a very limited number, mainly oak, beech, elm (*Ulmus procera*) and ash (*Fraxinus excelsior*). This simplicity in the planting maintained the characteristic simplicity of the trees of the vegetation cover of the natural forest which once covered most of the landscape. When selecting species for new planting in the countryside, it is wise to reflect on its present serene appearance – if a large number of species had been used. On the Continent, the plains of the North were planted with many narrow woodlands and avenues, using poplar species which produced another kind of serene appearance (Fig. 11.5); the practice is continued in Holland today, although the careful selection of a particular poplar species or variety for each location avoids complete sameness: on heavy clay soils, *Populus serotina*; to face strong winds, *Populus robusta*; on sandy, loamy soils, *Populus marilandica*, and in stream valleys, *Populus gelrica*. Poplar species are, in general, regular in habit (especially the commercial strains) and thus are appropriate in appearance for the flat topography which, in

Fig. 11.5 The new town of Emmeloord in the North East Polder of Holland. The regular tree planting is suited to the flat topography.

turn, gave rise to the logical planning of straight roads and drainage canals and ditches.

11.2. Planting in rural areas

The countryside, as it exists today in many developed countries, has many types of vegetation, from the wild areas to the planted parklands and avenues of recent times. Planting of the former type is likely to mean nature reserves and the wild parts of national parks; in these landscapes new 'planting' should be restricted to thinning out woodland where it exists around car parks and field study centres (Fig. 11.6), and bringing out the shrub layer into the open as a groundcover to differentiate a land use from the surrounding landscape, with some changes in the species necessitated by the increased illumination. With grassed picnic areas and other similar spaces in woodland, the grass can be taken into the cleared edge (see Section 10.3), and replacement of trees in the future would need to be carried out by planting standard trees. These two examples illustrate the need for a sensitive approach when introducing land uses into natural and wild landscapes. Elsewhere in these landscapes, it is a matter of preserving the natural vegetation by controlled access.

Fig. 11.6 A natural woodland in the U.S.A. thinned for recreational purposes, but the future of the picnic area will depend upon new tree planting taking place because there will be no natural regeneration.

117

In some developed countries like Britain, the landscape of national park and regional recreation areas has been changed from its natural state to agricultural and afforested areas; the selection of tree and shrub species should accord with those native to the site or which have become part of the rural scene, and also those regenerating readily. For example, in Britain brambles and the dog rose (*Rosa canina*) on clay or clay/loam soils, or heathers and gorse on acid or sandy soils, are indicative of the kind of shrub planting for open areas. The coppicing technique at the boundary between open areas – for uses like car parks and picnicking – and woodland not only gives screening, but marks the areas as special uses in the countryside; but a design which produces the effect of glades in woodland can also be a good solution to the car parking problem. If shrub species related to the tree species of the locality are planted around the smaller land use areas in the countryside, the effect is to reduce the scale of the landscape. If willow trees are present, the grey sallow shrub (*Salix cinerea*) will give this reduction in scale, and the wild cherry similarly by the blackthorn shrub (*Prunus spinosa*).

Most of the planting in the countryside is functional, such as for shelter belts or stabilizing sand dunes by special afforestation techniques. With increased mobility and leisure, there is a growing demand for the amenity landscape, and if it has a semi-wild appearance, it will relate better to the large scale landscapes of agriculture and afforestation than the more consciously designed landscapes of the urban areas. A birch woodland with a bluebell groundcover, or a beech woodland with a sparse groundcover, have this character and are suitable for informal recreation such as might be associated with a country park.

The large areas of countryside used for agriculture establish a precedent which will influence the design of the landscape change and its planting. At the present time, the argument for replenishing the traditional woodland and hedgerow pattern of the countryside weighs strongly against its removal in order to increase the area devoted to a single cereal crop or pasture. The loss of the hedgerow elms has added weight to the argument and increased the need for a replanting policy to be set in motion with the utmost speed. But a speedier increase in the tree population is likely to come from a policy of grouping trees instead of single trees planted in hedgerows, and from planting around farm boundaries and in the many pockets of unused land. As a result of the experience of planting large numbers of elms in prominent places, followed by a rampant disease directed against them, the countryside will have to accept a greater range of species; at the same time, the recommendations made for following the traditional simplicity in species selection should be kept in mind.

Planting around buildings in the countryside has visual and functional advantages. A building or a small group of buildings can appear to have no connection with the countryside – merely being foreign objects and small in size compared with the extent of the landscape. Tree, and to a lesser degree shrub, planting which links a building visually to the hedgerow and woodland pattern (Fig. 11.7) overcomes this appearance of isolation. An exception is in the stone-wall landscape where a direct connection between the material of the building and the walls produces a visual relationship. The functional advantages of planting around buildings are shelter from the wind and privacy for the living area of the residents, the former function provided by tree and shrub species selected for their wind resistance characteristics (see Section 13.3) and their affinity with the local landscape, and the latter function by planting smaller species on the inside to accord with the domestic scale and environment, for example, crab apple trees, the guelder rose and *Rosa* spp.

In some parts of Britain particular tree and shrub species have become associated with buildings in the countryside, such as Scots pine (*Pinus sylvestris*) in upland areas and beech in lowland areas; these associations should not be disregarded in planting around buildings in the countryside. When buildings appear unrelated to the local landscape because the materials and forms are those associated with mechanical processes, tree planting is particularly helpful in partially screening where even the most careful siting of the building in the topography is unable to produce a satisfactory result. The design of the planting is aided by studying sections drawn through the existing vegetation and the topography between surrounding places from which the building can be seen, and the building site, in order to ascertain the best places to plant for screening purposes. Tree and shrub planting at selected places in the surrounding landscape can reduce the number of times an observer sees the particular building by obstructing his view at close range.

The siting of planting in the countryside should take into account the land uses and a successful result is likely to come from a realistic and sensitive compromise between the visual, the ecological and the land use points of view. The visual or appearance point of view is the most difficult to substantiate to everybody in a convincing way; there are, however, some principles concerning planting and topography which should be considered and may help to explain the importance of a good visual result.

The topography should always play a large part in siting tree groups and belts, and woodland and forest boundaries. Woodland planting on a hill should be seen to continue over the hill from all viewpoints and should not terminate half way up the hill, especially if the boundary is straight. Small mounds or hills can make an increased visual contribution if planted with trees, if the designer's intention is to increase the impression of height variation, instead of leaving the small mounds or hills to register as a topographical change. A line of trees following a boundary along a ridge line of the topography has often been acknowledged as an unsatisfactory element in the landscape. More questionable is the principle that planting in the surrounding landscape should be sited so that only one view of a distant hill in its entirety should be possible, though many partial glimpses are acceptable.

Fig. 11.7 The trees soften the change from the topography to the buildings.

Topography can vary the shadows cast by trees and tree groups in addition to the variations caused by the movement of the sun, and further variations occur from the accessible viewpoints. Similarly, indentations in the planting at the edges of tree belts and woodlands need consideration at the design stage in relation to orientation, and the formation of shade and shadow.

Traditionally in Britain, amenity areas in the countryside, such as the parklands, were often differentiated as landscapes from the surrounding agricultural areas by means of a belt of trees. Today, when the countryside is observed from many viewpoints by town dwellers as well as country folk, it does not seem logical for this visual distinction to remain in such a marked way. Thus, if an amenity area has a surrounding belt of trees which is linked to other planting in the surrounding landscape, the division into amenity and agricultural landscapes is less clear as regards appearance (Fig. 11.8). Even so, owners of rural estates may ask for some way in which their ownership can be expressed visually whilst maintaining continuity over the landscape; uniformity in tree species is one possibility, and the planting of only a particular species for short distances along the verges of every road entering the estate is another possibility.

11.3. Roads in rural areas

The design principles for roads in rural areas, and the planting associated with them, are somewhat different for the three grades – the inter city motorway type, the local road network, and the minor roads and lanes

Fig. 11.8 The amenity landscape around the medieval buildings in the centre of the picture is well linked to the planting in the surrounding agricultural landscape.

originally laid down for access to farms and hamlets. The last type, being narrow in width and not designed for speed, can usually become part of the agricultural field pattern by planting hedgerows on each side and occasional trees or groups in the hedgerows to continue the rhythm of the tree planting in the surrounding landscape. The local road requires a careful selection of tree and shrub species which accord closely with changes in the soil types and takes account of the native species and those species which have become associated with different localities. By following these principles, the planting contributes to the local road becoming an element of the landscape without undue visual impact. Roads are large in scale and thus planting should generally take place in groups rather than as single trees; also, group planting offers the advantage of mutual shelter in the establishment period.

Two different principles have been advanced for planting along motorways: first, because its function is to allow traffic to speed from one centre to another without access to the countryside through which it passes, the planting belongs to this single function and should not reflect the changing ecological conditions along the route; second, that the species should change with the ecology. Between these two opposed principles, it may be possible to find one or more species common to each ecological condition and to add to the plant list, for use along the whole length, introduced species which are able to survive in the different conditions. Planting design proposals along a motorway are helped when it is sited to accord with the landscape and not in such a way that it must always be hidden by the topography or by planting, because there will be places where planting would disturb the appearance of a landscape which acquires its beauty from the topography alone.

The international conference on 'Roads in the Landscape' at the University of Keele in 1967 produced some 'unofficial' standards affecting planting in the papers and discussion, particularly concerned with wind, snow and anti-dazzle. For example, it is important to study the behaviour of winds on and around roads; gaps in heavily wooded margins in exposed landscapes are likely to produce dangerous wind funnelling, but dispersed small groups of trees or narrow tree belts with limited shrub cover in the same situation are likely to reduce wind speed a little without noticeable funnelling. The tree belts, particularly those with a low shrub cover, should be set back about 25 to 30 m from the carriageway, and in this position they also help to reduce snow drifts. Safety and visibility considerations point to a clear area outside the carriageway before planting of at least 4 m for high speed roads and just over 2 m for slow speed roads.

Planting in the central reservation of a dual carriageway road can help to overcome the dazzle problem from the headlights of advancing vehicles, but a complete solution requires also a contribution from the design of the road in relation to the topography and in the amount of land required. A central reservation, at least 2.5 m in width, is necessary for the minimum kind of planting; this narrow width is too restrictive for tree planting (Fig. 11.9),

Fig. 11.9 Although this is an attractive road landscape, the central reservation is too narrow for the growth of trees.

exposes shrubs to the full effect of salting against frost, and hence cannot be considered as practicable. A width of 20 m is the measure of the land required between the carriageways to give the effect of the surrounding landscape continuing across the road. On straight stretches, it is unnecessary for planting to be continuous; gaps of 30 to 50 m can be left, but only if there is no problem from the wind conditions referred to previously. When the road curves or on gradients, planting should be continuous in the central reservation, and the species selected should be able to grow to more than the 1.8 m in height necessary for the level straight lengths.

Considerations of scale should enter into planting decisions for roads. If tall forest trees like beech or the dawn redwood (*Metasequoia glyptostroboides*) are planted for central reservation or roadside planting, a width of at least 30 m of ground is needed to give trees of this size an appropriate setting. Autumn leaf fall on to the carriageways is less of a problem if the trees have their own generous plot of land.

Many new roads through the countryside cut across field boundaries, leaving isolated triangles of land. Sometimes, these small plots can be added to an adjoining field, but they can also be used for small plantations which add to the road planting, though it may necessitate purchasing more land for the road than the bare minimum. These small plantations add variety to the road landscape and accord with the point frequently made that a road with variety from many changes of direction helps to maintain the driver's concentration. Plantations at right angles to a road (Fig. 11.10), and possibly

Fig. 11.10 The considerable contribution made by a small belt of trees at right angles to a road.

linking with existing plantations or isolated buildings well back from the road, help to break the long distance view along straight stretches.

The motorway type of road junction occupies a large area of land and its visual impact on the landscape is very considerable unless the topography is able to 'absorb' the slip roads and under- and overpasses. Provided visibility is maintained at critical places, this type of junction, including the 'clover leaf', can be planted as though it lies within a woodland although, unless large woodlands exist in the surrounding landscape, the new planted element can look out of place. The surrounding landscape should determine the landscape design of the junction – in an open landscape, grading operations to the topography with shrub or groundcover planting, and in a hedgerow landscape a combination of grading, tree groups and shrub cover, are likely to produce acceptable results (Fig. 11.11). The roundabout type of junction permits little in the way of variation from its circular form and, in some ways, poses the most difficult planting problem; provided the criteria limiting the height of planting within certain sight lines are observed[3], any deviation which can be achieved from a perfect circle facilitates the design of planting in a manner which accords with the surrounding landscape. The right-angle junction on one side of a road usually involves adjusting and extending existing planting, again within sight line limits.

The technical problems of road planting include the disturbance of the soil, erosion on cuttings and embankments, and pollution and salting, which result from the construction and use of roads. The effects of salting are difficult to rectify, but planting should be kept at least 5 m from the edge of a

Fig. 11.11 The numerous woodlands around this complicated junction of road and rail systems are invaluable in its appearance in the landscape.

carriageway in order to avoid damage; even so, there is a risk that the cumulative effects can be present up to a distance of 9 m.

The nature of a modern road makes maintenance difficult without stringent safety precautions. Thus, planting techniques should be at a high level to give the trees and shrubs a good start, especially providing adequate pockets of good soil and a stable habitat until the root systems have become established. Reasonable freedom from competition in the early years is also important.

Planting along roads over the last two decades has been, with derelict landscape reclamation projects, one of the largest contributions to the tree and shrub population of the countryside in Britain – always excepting afforestation planting; the experience gained in these operations has been invaluable for successful planting. Whereas planting with seedling trees, two or three years old, is normal practice in commercial forestry, the exposure on many road embankments and cuttings, and the importance of creating an early visual impression, has led to the planting of young whip trees of some four or five years growth and which are comparatively economical. The

125

standard tree with its supporting stake is a more expensive proposition, and ranges from about 2 m above ground at planting to 4 or 5 m for large standards. Standards are best kept for places where quick effect is more urgent, such as junctions and associated facilities like car parks and picnic areas.

11.4. Roads in urban areas

The many different types of roads in urban areas suggest different planting policies. With urban motorways, ring roads and parkways it would seem logical for the planting associated with them to have an identity and not be merely a continuation of the planting policy of the surrounding urban areas, although both policies should have sufficient in common to associate them with the town as a whole – there might be, for example, two significant tree species common to the planting of many public areas.

Urban roads, which are not specifically access roads through the town like the urban motorways, are better planted in relation to the immediate environment; the formal environment of a complex of civic buildings justifies the formal planting of one species of tree at equal intervals, while a road bordering a public park should have planting related to the large trees of the park. An exception is that major local roads could have their own planting scheme to mark their importance as the route from which access to the residential units is arranged, but the relationship between the planting of the major local road and the residential units should have a similar common factor as with the urban motorways and the town.

In general, the planting policy should reduce the visual impact of roads in urban areas, and this can be achieved by large-scale planting in plots of land at intervals through the town (Fig. 11.12), rather than by small trees following the line of a road, which only emphasizes the appearance of a road. Preferably, the tree groups should be sited, and their form or outline designed, so that the observer senses a visual relationship between them, and that 'endless' views are terminated, unless a particular view is significant. The planting of roads in urban areas should contribute to the urban scene as a whole and avoid expressing in a visual way the ideas conjured up by 'Cherry Tree Avenue' or 'Laburnum Grove'; the best place for small trees, usually of exotic origin, is within the private garden.

Planting along roads sometimes interferes with a view valued by the occupiers of nearby buildings. The view can be kept open by avoiding the planting of shrubs and by removing the lower branches of the trees as they grow; interest at the lower level can be kept by grass species suitable for shade conditions (see Section 10.3.), with bulbs 'naturalizing'. Shrub planting over large areas has rarely been used in urban road schemes (Fig. 11.13), although it has considerable visual interest if, as with perennials, the selected species do not include plants with spectacular flowers which tempt the motorist to take his eyes off the road. Road widening and new roads in built-up areas often leave ends of buildings exposed, so that an ugly street

Fig. 11.12 Substantial groups of trees in association with urban roads make a greater impact in the urban landscape than small trees following the line of roads.

Fig. 11.13 An example of shrub planting in association with an urban road, and of sufficient size to make the necessary visual impact.

scene is created; in these circumstances, tree planting can be successful as a visual screen, although the time taken for the trees to reach an adequate size, compared with the likelihood of the exposed building being replaced, are matters that will enter into the decision.

For the technical reasons of leaf fall, shade and possible damage to buildings by roots, trees need an adequate amount of land in which to grow. When tall buildings are present, an adequate amount of land is also necessary in order that large trees can be planted at a distance – large trees are the dominants of the forest and should not be demoted by the dwarfing effect from too close an association with tall buildings. It is not possible to be precise about the extent of tree roots and thus possible damage to services and foundations, because soil and water table conditions are variable; the radius of the crown of a mature tree has sometimes been quoted as the extent of root growth, and an average extent of 1.3 times the height of a tree as another measurement[4]. Within the area defined by these dimensions, it would be prudent to safeguard services and building foundations. Trees having a fastigiate or columnar habit are useful choices for restricted places – many common trees have fastigiate varieties such as beech (*Fagus sylvatica 'Dawyck'*) and oak (*Quercus petraea 'Columnaris'*).

Tree planting is possible in paved areas, using tree grids and gravelled or soiled areas around the base of the tree, but tree guards are likely to be necessary for protection from pedestrians, particularly when the paved surface continues right up to the trunk with the use of a metal or concrete grid.

11.5. Planting in urban areas

Planting along roads in urban areas often merges with the planting of residential, shopping and industrial areas, and with civic sites; this is particularly apparent with culs de sac and pedestrianized streets. Apart from the many possibilities with tree and shrub planting in the streets and squares, and in relation to buildings[5], tree belts and groups contribute in a small way to reducing urban noise and pollution, and are important for shelter from winds.

In the residential areas, traditional planting policies included the densely planted common garden in the green spaces of squares and crescents, but without any planting specifically associated with the houses. While a criticism is that the dense planting reduced the amount of space available to the residents, the contrast between the unrelieved building facades and the mass of vegetation produced a highly regarded urban landscape.

The Garden City movement led to a new planting policy along the streets and in the gardens which, at maturity, produced a landscape looking almost as 'green' as a woodland, and with the houses mostly hidden from view. If this policy is to be entirely successful, there must be some form of control or agreement about the planting in the private gardens. It has the merit of reducing the visual impact of any shortcomings in architectural quality and neighbourliness. A similar result is achieved by each house plot contained in a pocket surrounded by tall shrubs which cut off the view of the roofs of houses from most ground level viewpoints.

If the layout of a residential area is a formal pattern of roads and buildings, there is a good reason for the tree and shrub planting to be arranged in blocks which accord with the size and position of the buildings. Usually with residential areas, informal planting is more successful, provided the mixture of species remains constant, because it gives some variation and individuality to the immediate landscape; the experimental work in Holland (see Fig. 11.5) incorporating wild plants growing freely takes the idea of the relationship between the house and the immediate landscape outside the garden much further by incorporating wild plants which are not restricted to specific flower beds[6]. It is the climate in Britain which sets the difficult problem of planting urban areas in such a way that the inhabitants are physically involved with it, instead of being merely spectators; for example, close proximity with vegetation often means being in the shade – pleasant enough in a hot climate, but rarely welcome in cool temperate climates.

Tree planting is a very important element in urban areas (Fig. 11.14); visually, trees have a scale relationship with many buildings, apart from tall blocks, and, once established, they require little maintenance apart from topping and lopping if they or the buildings have been incorrectly sited or from vandalism. The shade effect of trees and the use of the ground beneath them limits maintenance operations. Shrubs are a little more demanding in

Fig. 11.14 The trees in this picture give shade to the play area in hot weather and reduce the visual interference of the fencing.

maintenance, but they can be sited to divert people away from areas which are easily damaged, and for this purpose vigorous and thorny species like *Berberis* and shrub roses are often recommended. Planting, however, is not always necessary in a landscape and might take away the effect of a natural or artificial landform, particularly in flat landscapes where even small topographical differences are visually important. Continuous planting of trees and shrubs is, however, valuable in corridors which connect the centre of an urban area with the countryside, because linear planting is successful in encouraging wildlife to penetrate into cities for our enjoyment and as members of the living landscape. It is regrettable, however, that this kind of dense planting may have to be avoided because it creates hidden pockets for criminal action.

In the smaller public open spaces, trees with a widely-spaced branch system and light leaf texture, e.g. birch and ash, are preferable to densely branched and vegetated trees because of the feeling of space they create (Fig. 11.15), and the surrounding urban scene is always partly visible – otherwise the open space may seem isolated. Dense shrub planting can, however, be used to create sheltered places with reasonable privacy.

The planting design of a large urban park is a more complicated problem, and involves a policy decision whether the park should be cut off from the surrounding streets and buildings with an enclosing belt, or whether the planting should connect them (Fig. 11.16), with perhaps vistas along a street and into the park and dense tree planting to screen the less attractive parts of

Fig. 11.15 Trees and shrubs with a sparse branch system are well suited to small open spaces in urban areas.

130

Fig. 11.16 Tree planting on the boundary of a public path in the U.S.A. which relates to the buildings of the town rather than to the informal planting of the park.

the urban scene. There is also the policing problem, one solution being 'open' planting at an unfenced periphery, but denser planting towards the middle and enclosed by railings and gates locked at dusk.

Two levels of planting are needed in urban parks: first, the structural planting which contributes to the arrangement of the spaces for different uses and is best selected from one list of suitable species, and second, the smaller scale 'ornamental' planting within the spaces and which has the structural planting as a background and setting for the visual effects of species selected from several different lists (Fig. 11.17). Another planting policy is the urban forest in which the various park uses, like games, water recreation and entertainments are located in glades. The urban environment around an urban forest gives rise to different atmospheric conditions than the rural forest and will mean some variation in species.

Planting in beds and borders will often be expected in urban areas, and is not out of place in the right situation; principles indicating how beds and borders may be incorporated in landscapes are outlined in Section 10.7, but in the scale of urban parks, the smaller plants should be set in 'pockets' among the larger plants of a basic structure of planting of the bed or border. There is often a place in urban areas for planting in pots, both temporary and permanent, and usually in association with paving and hard landscape; with this kind of planting, seasonal interest can be extended beyong the period possible with plants grown from seed or seedlings *in situ*. The principles

Fig. 11.17 Small scale planting in a space in a public park formed by the 'structural' tree planting pattern.

132

relating to colour and texture (Sections 4.5 to 4.7) can be applied to the design of planting in pots without the limitations of normal habitat conditions.

11.6. Planting in industrial sites

There are three categories of industrial site, each requiring a different planting policy; these are described as the site in the countryside, the urban site, and sites which are being reclaimed from derelict and mineral extraction landscapes.

In rural areas, many of the principles stated for the planting of small woodlands, tree belts and groups of trees are relevant (Section 11.2), but with emphasis on integrating the industry into the countryside; often the Planning Authority will make screening a condition of approval. The best planting design will usually connect the new proposals with existing tree groups and woodlands in the surrounding landscape, and also will arrange the planting so that the spaces created are similar in size to the field pattern or other division of the landscape. Planting in the areas around an industrial site is advantageous when close to well-used viewpoints, as with a group of ten trees, underplanted with shrubs, which can hide a large building some distance away from positions within a considerable area on the side of the planting away from the building. Many industrial buildings are too large for tree planting to serve as a complete screen, but when associated with earthworks and offsite planting, their visual impact is reduced. The colours of the trees and the buildings have a bearing upon the incorporation of the latter into the landscape, although seasonal variation of the vegetation has to be taken into account. The paint or materials' colours of the buildings and mechanical plant might be predominantly 'steel blue', with lesser surfaces of contrasting 'lime green' and 'rose madder'; trees completing this colour effect are, for example, *Acer platanoides 'Crimson King'* and the white poplar, with the red stemmed dogwood (*Cornus alba 'Sibirica'*) and *Kerria japonica* as shrubs effective in Winter. Planting design solutions of this kind may not always accord with a design based upon the local ecology, but the requirement for a visually acceptable industrial landscape should be matched by the necessary maintenance cost which industry should be prepared to meet.

Small scale planting on large industrial sites should relate to the hedgerow scale and range of species rather than the garden scale, even if there is no surrounding landscape, except when the planting can only be seen from within the site. Carefully mown grass lawns are also better arranged in the same way, except for the main entrance to the site, leaving the larger grass areas scythed occasionally with the dual advantage of saving on maintenance costs and in scale and sympathy with industrial complexes.

The emphasis in planting design for most industrial sites in urban areas is on screening with trees and shrubs, especially when the buildings and mechanical plant are not visually acceptable (Fig. 11.18). But when

133

Fig. 11.18 Before and after photographs of a gravel pit showing the effect of a tree-planted screen (courtesy of The Sand and Gravel Association).

screening is unnecessary, planting tree and shrub belts as a continuation of the form of the buildings until they link visually with the form of buildings on adjoining sites is an acceptable arrangement, and often preferable on the limited area of industrial sites in urban areas to informal planting which tries to give them a parkland character. Tree species which are suitable for creating a visual link between the form of buildings should have a regular habit with each tree looking like its neighbour and equally spaced – some poplars and conifers fall into this category (Fig. 11.19).

Planting, which is large enough in scale to be associated with the scale of modern industry, needs adequate room. It is also at risk from future expansion of the industry unless the layout of the site is arranged so that the essential planting is in positions which would present difficulties for any expansion, such as a part of the site lying below the level of the sewers. Even with a landscape condition on the planning permission there seems to be no guarantee that a future application for expansion will be turned down.

Mention has been made of the scale of the planting on industrial sites. Nevertheless, in urban areas, it may be necessary to reduce this scale at the site boundary if the surroundings have a domestic scale of planting. Planting to reduce dust and smoke is helpful and requires a study of the local climate and the microclimatic variations resulting from the industrial buildings and mechanical plant and the on-site planting.

Planting design for the reclaimed derelict and mineral extraction landscapes has, as a major objective, the re-establishment of a fertile

134

Fig. 11.19 Trees when used to form a visual link between a formal arrangement of buildings are effective if planted in a regular manner.

landscape, and for which research findings and experience are available[7]. When the proposal is the reinstatement of a previous agricultural landscape, a successful landscape design policy follows the field pattern of the surrounding landscape so that it is difficult to identify where the reclamation began and ended, even though the topography is different because of the bulk of waste material. In the case of an active mineral extraction site, a phased planting policy, relating to the surrounding landscape and the need for screening, is likely to be required. In the case of the surface extraction of sand or gravel, the new low levels in high water table areas mean a wetland landscape which is a challenge to the designer to bring the wetland and surrounding dryland plantings together in an acceptable manner (see Section 10.5.).

The usual practice today with landscape reclamation projects is to include grading operations to make the appearance of the topography more acceptable and its gradients more useful. There are still projects where grading is not in the design brief for the reclamation, and reliance has to be placed almost entirely upon the planting – often into the waste material (Fig. 11.20). In these circumstances, it is advisable to phase the proposals so that planting commences in those places where vegetation is beginning to establish naturally; by increasing moisture availability through minor grading operations and fertility with some form of manure, stable areas of vegetation can be established which may increase in area naturally or create shelter for future planting. The expensive alternative is to plant the entire

135

Fig. 11.20 Planting in association with a reclaimed landscape in the brown coal area of West Germany.

area with seedling trees and allow them to flourish or fail in accordance with the favourable and unfavourable conditions, and gradually add planting in the unfavourable areas as the conditions improve with growth in the favourable areas. If the derelict landscape is the 'hill and dale' type, and if grading to a level topography is not possible, the ridges of the 'hills' will be the most suitable places for planting, because the bottoms of the 'dales' may be waterlogged.

Reservoirs can be classed as a form of industrial landscape, usually in the countryside, and they have their own special planting problems and conditions, as well as those already discussed for waterside habitats (see Section 10.5). There are, for example, the problems set by the new water table and the seasonal draw-down (Fig. 11.21). The policy often adopted for some of the older reservoirs in Britain was enclosing them with coniferous planting; this policy was directed to the separation of a reservoir from the surrounding landscape and restricting public access to potential attractive places for recreation, and it emphasized the harsh effect of the draw-down. The new enlightened policy takes account of the tree and shrub species in the surrounding landscape, and exploits the variations in the steepness of the banks and their height in relation to the water levels in order that 'dry land' species are planted close to the water in some places, while 'wet land' species penetrate between 'dry land' areas in other places. An essential exercise to carry out before designing planting around proposed reservoirs is to observe how the different water levels will cut through existing woodlands and hedgerows by plotting the level on a map, followed by visits to the reservoir

Fig. 11.21 The tree belts extending down to the reservoir in the distance in this example assist with the 'draw down' problem common to reservoirs.

site to observe where these cuts will occur. This study of the effect of the high water level is helped by observing the swing of a dumpy level set up at points on the future margin; this exposes places where new planting, or even additional felling of trees, will be needed to reduce the effects of the water at its various levels.

References
[1] Miles, Roger (1967), *Forestry in the English Landscape*, Faber & Faber, London. Pages 175–8 give further information on the appearance of tree species in forests.
[2] The Game Conservancy, Fordingbridge, Hants., England, publishes a comprehensive list of tree and shrub species for game bird habitats.
[3] *Roads in Urban Areas* (1966) and *Layout of Roads in Rural Areas* (1968), H.M.S.O., London.
[4] Yeager, A. F. (1935), Root systems of certain trees and shrubs grown on prairie soils, *Journal of Agricultural Research* **51**, No. 12.
[5] Ministry of Housing & Local Government (1958), *Trees in Town and City*, H.M.S.O., London, for numerous illustrations of trees growing in different urban situations and comment thereon.
[6] Cole, L. and Keen, C. (1976), Dutch techniques for the establishment of natural plant communities in urban areas, *Journal of the Institute of Landscape Architects,* **116**, 31–34.
[7] Hackett, B. (ed.) (1971–2), *Landscape Reclamation*, Vols. I and II, I.P.C. Science and Technology Press Ltd., Guildford.

CHAPTER 12

Planting for cover and food bondage

In Section 8.2 reference was made to the links between the flora and the fauna in a biotic community; in particular, the vegetation is critical in one way or another to the existence of animals, birds and insects. Vegetation is a vital link in the food chain in addition to its contribution to the habitat conditions of sheltered niches for bringing up new generations and for protection against the climate and attack. Concerning the conservation of wildlife as generally understood, the berries produced by some trees and shrubs, and the insects and larvae who inhabit their leaves and branches, provide the food supply; trees like the evergreen holly provide Winter food and early shelter for nesting before the deciduous trees come into leaf.

12.1. Wildlife and types of planting

It would be a very difficult exercise to prepare a planting plan which ensured that a particular wildlife population would develop, but diversity of species and types of vegetation, and in the way in which it is arranged in a planting design, is an essential prerequisite. The area and volume of planting is also important; a privet hedge (*Ligustrum vulgare*) alongside a paved backyard provides a limited habitat, but in order to encourage a range of wildlife, 0.45 hectares of landscape is the minimum for open and closed areas with some diversity in the vegetation, and is preferable to the same area in three or four separate plots. In order to provide diversity, the strata of vegetation, the groundcover, the shrubs and the trees, should be present in various combinations, and separately.

The edges of the closed canopy parts of a wildlife conservation area are the places where dense undercover vegetation will develop because there is shelter, adequate illumination and the competition from other species is only from the inside (Fig. 12.1). Thus, if a woodland wildlife area is bounded by open landscape, with little interference, the perimeter will be a valuable habitat. But if the perimeter is fenced against busy roads and paths, this advantage is reduced and the clearings within the area assume greater

Fig. 12.1 A copse or spinney planted as a habitat for game birds, but which has the ingredients for many species of wildlife.

importance. Deciduous woodlands provide a wider range of wildlife habitats than coniferous woodlands, but a mixed edge of deciduous and coniferous species to a coniferous woodland, of at least 10 m in width, can be valuable for wildlife.

Clearings in a wooded wildlife area are necessary in order to supplement these rich edges to the canopied parts, and also for the different ground flora of the clearings, which is likely to attract many insects, including butterflies. Grasses are the basis of the vegetation of the clearings, but there should also be various herb species. A favourable size of clearing which will give the maximum microclimatic benefit from all points of view (shelter, sunshine, warmth, air movement, etc), and is large enough to provide an alternative landscape for wildlife from the canopied areas around, is about 22 m across. Some management of cleared areas may be necessary unless the wildlife are able to control the growth of young seedling trees and shrubs, and one cut over the area in the month of May will enable the herb species to make some growth subsequently. If any ground-nesting birds are likely to be present, cutting should not take place until well into July at the earliest. An alternative method of control is to have a pattern of regularly mown paths and for the spaces between to be subject to various times and intervals of cutting so that there will always be some areas uncut over a full year.

If the vegetation of a wildlife area can be linked to other areas by means of hedgerows beside fields or paths or tree and shrub planting in linear 'strips' of grass, this helps to promote the movement of wildlife from one place to another, especially when the link commences in the countryside. For this purpose tall hedges, trimmed rather than cut back to a regular shape, are preferable to the formal closely-clipped hedge. Small trees which are not tall enough to form a canopy above normal disturbance by people and animals on the ground, and which do not have low side branches, are limited in forming wildlife habitats. A deciduous or mixed woodland with dense undercover and a canopy above normal disturbance often has the greatest number of birds' nests at just over 3 m above the ground; below and above this height, the number of nests diminishes rapidly. The pattern is, however, different in an area of open landscape with no dividing hedges, but trees at about 4 to 5 m intervals (such as in some open gardens in the U.S.A.), where the nests increase in numbers with the height above ground. Wildlife has proved to be fairly adaptable to noise and movement changes in the environment.

Coppicing (see Section 11.1) makes a favoured environment for wildlife because it allows greater illumination within the coppice than the close-canopy forest, and thus has a richer groundflora. Also, the mass of vertical shoots from each root system gives well screened niches for protection. Two tree species traditionally used for coppicing, however, are low in the list of trees acting as hosts for insects, these being hornbeam (*Carpinus betulus*) and sweet chestnut (*Castanea sativa*). Coppice with standards is another type of woodland management, with the advantage as a wildlife habitat that the vegetation and the shape and size of clear living spaces are more diverse and variable than with a pure coppice management policy. The pioneer and early stages of development of a woodland after clearance encourage a considerable wildlife population because the vegetation is dense until the growth of the large forest trees controls the under storey.

12.2. Management of planting

Neglected areas of green landscape have a considerable wildlife population which is an argument for leaving them in that state (Fig. 12.2); in particular, studies of neglected churchyards in urban areas show a wide range of bird and other forms of wildlife. In order to make the untidy vegetation more acceptable visually, some thinning and undercover clearance on the perimeter will usually suffice. Thinning and clearing in wildlife areas, however, should not be carried out in the nesting season, and it is an advantage to allow a few trees to grow to a very old age, leaving some dead wood for harbouring insects, provided they are not sources of disease. The growth of scrub vegetation on neglected grassland will encourage a wildlife population, but is likely to discourage butterflies. Also, the grouping of a number of vegetable garden plots into an allotment area has potential for wildlife if associated with tree planting and dividing hedges, although steps may have to be taken to protect some crops from birds and animals.

Fig. 12.2 Neglected areas often develop a vegetation cover which, in turn, encourages wildlife, as in this bomb damaged site in West Germany.

12.3. Plant species

Reference is made in the Appendix to lists of British plants which are useful in wildlife areas. Conifers do not come high up in such lists, but by including about 0.5 hectares of mountain ash (*Sorbus aucuparia*), birch, alder and hazel in each 5 hectares of coniferous planting, the necessary variety of insect life is likely to be present. The tree species most favoured by insects include oak, willows and poplars, but these species are unlikely to grow well in the conditions in which commercial coniferous forests are planted in Britain.

In the case of water-loving birds, the waterside planting (Fig. 12.3) for their food and protection should also be protected if people or animals have access; fencing is one method of protection, though planting shrubs with spikes or dense twigs on the land side is more likely to be visually acceptable in connection with a wildlife area. When the shoreline has indentations, these are useful places to plant because of the shelter which is both sought after by birds and is helpful to the establishment of the planting (see also Section 10.5). In order to provide the diversity of species and types of vegetation which is essential in planting for most wildlife areas, the depths of the water at the margin should vary (see Section 10.5), and some places along the margin should be low-lying to give a marsh habitat where plants like the common spike or marsh club rush (*Eleocharis palustris*) and the creeping buttercup (*Ranunculus repens*) can be grown. Tree species which have a food value and can be planted in the vicinity of areas for water-loving

Fig. 12.3 In the centre of this picture the young trees already provide shelter and food for wildlife around small ponds.

birds are the alder, birch and oak. Some places along the margin, particularly sheltered areas of sand or shingle, should be left devoid of vegetation for the birds to rest and preen their feathers.

  Prior to finalizing a planting design for a wildlife area, a valuable check on plant species is usually available from local experts at the local University or Natural History Society and, in Britain, from the regional office of the Nature Conservancy Council.

CHAPTER 13

Planting for environmental control

Planting is often grown in a landscape for a specific function instead of using an inorganic material, for example, a hedge instead of a brick wall around an orchard to reduce the effect of wind. There are many occasions when vegetation is visually more acceptable and less costly than brick or concrete, and can also influence the local environment, as well as the micro-environment of a small ownership, by its contribution to purifying and cooling the atmosphere in urban areas.

13.1. Planting and atmospheric purification

It is not possible to predict an exact purification or cooling result over a certain area of urban development from any given volume or leaf area of vegetation because of the variable movement of air from the countryside and across the urban area, and in view of the different levels of pollution in towns. It has been suggested that, if vegetation is the sole medium through which carbon dioxide is absorbed from, and oxygen given to, the atmosphere, each inhabitant would require 30 to 40 m² of green space, including trees and shrubs[1]. Given adequate private gardens with trees and shrubs in the residential areas and some street tree planting, this figure could well be halved for deciding upon the area of public landscape needed for atmospheric purification; the present level of pollution in towns from motor cars and industry would, however, suggest a figure of about 25 m² of public landscape backed up by private gardens. For this particular purpose of reducing atmospheric pollution, trees and shrubs add very considerably to the contribution of a grassed open space, and they are also useful in reducing dust and particles arising from combustion and industry.

Vegetation, as well as reducing atmospheric pollution, has a useful effect upon climate. A convincing comparison of the temperature difference between a planted area of urban landscape and a built-up central area is that, on average, for an area of the former type which is only in the 50–100 m width range, Summer temperatures are likely to be 3.5% lower with a 5%

increase in the relative humidity. If the planted areas can be arranged so that air currents from the countryside or from well planted residential areas pass through them into the central area, the lowered temperature will benefit the town as a whole.

13.2. Planting to control erosion

Vertical and lateral erosion are the two types of erosion which can be controlled by appropriate vegetational treatments, and unless they are controlled, the topographical, drainage, and vegetational aspects of the environment will change. The former results from the leaching of soluble nutrients downwards through the soil as in some upland areas in a wet climate and where the tree cover has been removed by grazing; the erosion can be held to a stable situation when a cover of heathland vegetation develops, although this is unlikely to have brought back a fertile topsoil. Techniques developed by foresters, which include deep ploughing, enable a successful restoration of a forest cover to take place (Fig. 13.1), and this would seem to be a more logical planting design solution than preserving the heathland, although the latter is a much admired landscape. In this instance, what seems to be the proper policy in landscape design conflicts with a strict planting design policy.

Lateral erosion leads to many different situations which can be controlled wholly or partly by planting and, if proof is required, a reminder about the Dust Bowl and eroded forests after clear felling in the U.S.A. is all that is necessary. Sheet erosion, as its name suggests, occurs over the whole surface of the eroding area, and can be gradual, such as a slow washing away on the

Fig. 13.1 Afforestation as an anti-erosion measure in Israel.

surface of exposed soil down a slope or, if the exposed soil is friable and the slope is steep, the effect can be dramatic. There is also the effect of wind – dramatic with pure sand soils and cumulative in dry spells on 'average' soils when a cover of vegetation is absent. The establishment of a permanent cover of vegetation which does not lead to soil deterioration is the natural solution, but when the land is to be worked with annual cropping, and thus periods of soil exposure, a system of shelter planting mitigates wind blow. Also, strips of a permanent vegetation cover, like permanent grassland, contain the washing away of soil to distant places. There are other methods of controlling lateral erosion which are not directly concerned with planting, such as terracing and parallel ditches running with the contours at about 6 m intervals to control the washing away of the soil. Structural methods are also used, as well as planting, to control slip on steep slopes [2].

When the slope and soil conditions are not too difficult and sheet erosion is gradual, grass seeding is effective and can be supplemented by tree and shrub planting. More difficult conditions require the use of special techniques like netting, mulching, turfing and lines of shrub or tree cuttings from easily propagated species driven into the slope at intervals – willow species have produced good results for this technique.

Wind blown erosion of the sand from coastal areas on to fertile land involves the special techniques of developing littoral dunes (Fig. 13.2) as a structural protection, brushwood thatching of the ground prior to planting tree seedlings and the planting of marram grass (*Ammophila arenaria*) as planting techniques.

The designer will, however, need to consider these areas subject to

Fig. 13.2 First stage planting of sand dunes for future development as grassland.

erosion as planted areas in the landscape, and the dilemma with heathland and the tree cover has already been mentioned. In the case of slopes, if they are steeper than is generally accepted for most purposes, say steeper than 1 in 7, tree and shrub planting is appropriate, not only because it is usually acceptable in the appearance of the landscape, but because it limits access to an area too steep for normal use. The advantages of slopes in making planting more effective are referred to in Section 10.2, but when slopes are in a large scale rural landscape or alongside a river or a road, compared with a private garden or small urban open space, the planting should not markedly change from that in the surroundings and do no more than indicate the change between level and sloping ground.

The plants which invade steep slopes are usually those requiring only comparatively infertile conditions of rapid run off, soil washing, or exposed subsoil in cuttings for road construction (Fig. 13.3). Typical species in Britain are gorse and broom which give a low shrub cover with grasses and wild herbs. The invasion of tree species is associated with more fertile conditions. If we consider a shrub cover of a steep slope, compared with a tree cover, as elements in the appearance of landscape, shrubs tend to emphasize the slope, while trees make a slope less prominent because of the varied silhouette where the trees rise above the crest of the slope (Fig. 13.4).

The logical planting design for a steep slope of considerable length, when the soil conditions are uniform, is to keep this uniformity. But if this is considered too monotonous, changes in the species should merge one into

Fig. 13.3 Planting to stabilize a sloping bank with shrubs, perennials and grass species from the native vegetation.

146

Fig. 13.4 The shrubs emphasize the lower part of the slope while the trees make the slope less prominent.

the other along the slope and not up the slope. The tree species along the crest can be selected to give some variation in the silhouette, if this is the right solution bearing in mind the tree belt and woodland silhouettes in the surrounding landscape. When a slope is orientated favourably, and the slope and soil conditions are favourable, the planting can be designed to give sheltered places at the base for grasses and herbs – further up the slope would restrict normal viewing of these sheltered places. But in the smaller scale landscapes where slopes may occur in urban areas, this change in the planting, especially if provided by beds of 'garden' plants, will disturb the contrasting effect of the steep slope with the level topography around.

Slopes which have been recently cultivated or have a newly prepared seed bed are subject to rill erosion when there has been heavy rainfall. With rill erosion, small channels are cut into the surface of the soil, and produce a pattern in miniature like the streams and tributaries of a river. If the slope is to be planted with shrubs to form a complete cover, it is advisable to grow a temporary grass cover which will disappear as the shrubs close in or with regular maintenance; with tree planting the grass cover is likely to be permanent. The timing of the seeding operation is important, and with moist clement weather a sufficient grass cover may develop before rill erosion sets in. A safeguard is to form small ditches at about 10 to 15 m centres, parallel with the contours, and connected to temporary drainage ditches at the

147

Fig. 13.5 Before and after photographs of a gulley showing the anti-erosion planting.

boundary of the slope; these ditches slow down the intensity of the run off sufficiently to allow the grass to develop, unless an exceptional storm occurs. Subsequently the ditches are filled in and seeded, and tree and shrub planting can take place.

Gulley erosion is the most spectacular type and the most serious in the short term (Fig. 13.5). It occurs when the eroding of the surface extends below the resistant organic layer of topsoil; once below this layer, the washing away of subsoil can form deep gulleys of V or U section very quickly. One effect of gulley erosion which has to be taken into account with planting proposals is the lowering of the water table around the gulley. Bearing in mind that many quick growing tree and shrub species are moisture-loving, it is advisable to combine a diversionary surface drainage system with small level channels around the head of the gulley to provide moisture for the plants. The head of the gulley is the position where stability must be achieved to prevent further cutting back up the slope, and unless the remedial measures are structural, it is the position where planting must be established successfully. Willow species, both tree and shrub, alder and poplar have proved their worth in these conditions, and should be planted closely and deeply in rows along the contours so that they form barriers to run off and will knit together the soil. Grass seeding of coarse, quick growing species is an additional safeguard. The second stage of planting takes place in the gulley itself, and once established a future decision can be made as to whether to fill in the gulley gradually over several years so that the vegetation is not submerged in one operation, or whether to leave the vegetated gulley as a stable channel to drain the whole area in combination with new diversionary channels around the head of the gulley.

13.3. Planting and microclimate

The major influences upon the microclimatic variations from the local climate stem from topographical effects like valleys orientated so that they modify the direction of the wind and plateaux bordered by slopes so that frost gathers at the bottom. Nevertheless, vegetation is important in its influence upon microclimate.

The effects and design of shelter belt planting are well documented, particularly in relation to agriculture and the countryside[3, 4]. Considered as a planting design problem, the shelter belt planted only with coniferous or deciduous species is not so effective all round as the mixed belt which allows some passage of wind through in the Winter and early Spring to dry out the ground, with sufficient illumination for a shrub cover to give shelter at or near the ground. A mixture of trees and shrubs with deciduous, coniferous and evergreen species gives a range of visual possibilities, and may link better with established woodlands in the vicinity (Fig. 13.6). The temptation to have smaller trees at the sides of a shelter belt for appearance reasons has to be resisted because the sheltering effect is lessened, but planting some

Fig. 13.6 A newly planted shelter belt in Holland.

species with a light branch system, interplanted with tall shrubs, at the sides will reduce the box-like effect.

Planting around all sides of a sheltered area can be varied to accord with the wind pattern (Fig. 13.7). If the cold Winter winds come from the North and North East, densely planted shelter belts are advisable on these sides, and if the warm Summer winds come from the South and South East, an open belt of a single row of trees on the other sides would give some shelter whilst allowing the movement of air on hot days. Variety in shelter belt planting can also be achieved without destroying its unity by varying the width, so that for the boundary of a farm holding, 7 or 8 rows of trees are planted at 1.5–2 m apart; for Winter feeding of livestock out of doors, 5–8 rows; for a field with signs of wind erosion, 4–6 rows; for a field in general use, 3–5 rows, and for a garden or orchard, 1–3 rows (Fig. 13.8).

If snow drifting is known to occur most frequently from a particular direction, a 100 m wide shelter belt will trap most of the snow drift within its boundaries if the groundcover is low for some distance inside. In hot climates, the design and arrangement of belts enclosing small spaces like gardens and paddocks should allow the movement of air, otherwise the protected area will be appreciably warmer during the day than the local climate.

Shelter belts and hedgerows can hold up the passage of cold air and form frost pockets in the topographical situation described earlier, unless sited with this possibility in mind, and planned so that 'concealed' gaps occur

Fig. 13.7 Mixed land uses of almost equal areas of forestry and pasture in Switzerland, the former providing shelter for the latter.

Fig. 13.8 When shelter belts are reduced to the minimum, great care is needed to relate them to the landscape because of their prominence against the open landscape.

which would allow the slow passage of cold air under calm conditions. Dense shelter belts around frost sensitive areas like orchards can be sited so that any down slope drifting of cold air is diverted around them.

13.4. Planting and noise reduction

With the increase in noise in towns and along roads in the countryside, it has been disappointing to find that trees and shrubs have only a minor effect as sound barriers compared with earth mounds and structures[5]. Planting which includes both trees and shrubs, with at least one third as evergreens, produces the best result in noise reduction; if the source of sound is well above ground level, grass is better at sound absorption than a hard surface. An indication of the effect of 30 m width of dense vegetation is given by the reduction by 5 dB of a source of noise at a frequency of 4000 Hz, and by 2 dB of a source at a frequency of 1000 Hz; this reduction, however, is not very significant when the noise level of a central area road in a town is in the 80–90 dB range. There is, however, a psychological effect upon awareness of noise when dense planting lies between the source and the listener. A green urban landscape of groups of trees and shrubs in a grass lawn would need to be at least 360 m across before people in the centre could enjoy a reasonable degree of quietude from traffic roads at the boundaries, and this would not dispose of the traffic hum.

Only in planting designs that have a purely visual purpose can it be said that planting does not perform a function in environmental control.

Reference in previous Chapters to planting for wildlife habitats, for maintaining or improving soil fertility, and for anti-glare purposes on roads, indicates the important role that planting plays in making the landscape a congenial living place.

References
[1] Bernatzky, A. (1958), Die Beeinflussung des Stadtklimas durch Grünanlagen, *Stadtehygiene.*
[2] Hackett, Brian (1971), *Steep Slope Landscapes*, Oriel Press, Newcastle-upon-Tyne.
[3] Caborn, J. M. (1965), *Shelterbelts and Windbreaks*, Faber & Faber, London.
[4] Le Sueur, A. D. C. (1951), *Hedges, Shelterbelts and Screens*, Country Life, London.
[5] Beck, G. (1965), *Pflanzen als Mittel zur Lärmbekämpfung*, Putzer-Verlag G.M.B.H. & Co. K.G., West Berlin. A research publication on the sound reducing effects of various species of tree and shrub.

CHAPTER 14

Planting design for easy management

There are two distinct operations concerned in the development of planting after the initial sowing of seed or the planting of root systems and bulbs which involve: first, protection against wear and tear, and second, the maintenance work of grass cutting, weeding, pruning, etc. The design policy of the landscape and the planting can reduce the cost of both operations; for example, if the landscape comprises a large grass 'prairie' with many wildflowers, maintained by limiting grazing to the Autumn, and in the Summer there are many visitors, excessive use and thus damage to the 'prairie' vegetation could be reduced by a landscape design based on a pattern of graded mounds encouraging people to follow the route between them.

14.1. Wear and tear

Damage to planted and seeded areas, which is not by intent but results from a large number of people using the areas (Fig. 14.1), can be avoided by the more drastic step of disallowing access. This policy would not be in line with the idea of people becoming involved with landscape in the same way that birds, animals and insects are members of the total landscape (see Section 11.5). Limiting access is, of course, necessary in the early stage of the development of a newly planted landscape and is usually arranged by means of temporary fences until the seeding and planting has grown sufficiently to be able to withstand reasonable use by people. Also, the excessive use by people of routes across sensitive areas which were not envisaged at the planning and design stage may have to be controlled by fencing or alternative access arrangements.

A more satisfactory result than fencing sensitive areas is achieved by planting which influences people to by-pass them; strong and spiky plants (Fig. 14.2) like several of the barberries (*Berberis* spp.) or brambles planted closely will protect sensitive tree and shrub areas – even so, they themselves may need temporary protection until they are established. The technique of

Fig. 14.1 An example of accepting the inevitable on a campus in the U.S.A. by providing footpaths for the routes people will surely take, and thus reducing wear and tear on the grass, and damage to the young trees.

Fig. 14.2 'Spiky' shrubs which allow vision across the landscape but ensure privacy for the ground floor rooms.

155

'coppicing' trees and shrubs in the Nursery at the seedling, whip and small standard stages produces plants with several stems rising from the stool; these have a greater resistance factor than young plants with a single stem, and form a 'mesh' of branches and leaves more quickly.

The planting of quick and prolifically-growing species, not only reduces the time before a landscape begins to acquire a mature appearance, but somehow gives the impression that the plants have taken over their territories in the landscape while leaving other areas for use by people. Most shrubs take only 5 years or so to acquire a mature appearance, whereas with trees the period may be 20 or many more years. Thus, a phased planting design with the trees as the ultimate dominants planted among shrubs, and the latter removed as the trees acquire a dominant position, allows the landscape to appear established until the designer's intention of a grass landscape with single trees and groups of trees can be realized.

The example given of grading a site to encourage access through it along the valleys between mounds can be taken a stage further by elevating the planting above the normal level by means of retaining walls. Another deterrent for preventing damage to the planting is for the footpaths through a site to have a strip of loose pebbles between the walking surface and the planting which is not very comfortable to the feet; this device has worked well in some parklands where large stones placed around tree trunks have reduced damage to the bark by cattle. In a similar manner, a landscape design which provides for an area of water between people and the planted area is very effective, although expensive unless the water body exists or is part of a proposal included for other reasons.

With some kinds of planting people will seek close contact in order to experience the maximum pleasure; this should be accepted and easy access provisions will minimize damage. A large bed of many varieties of hybrid tea rose will tempt people to walk into the bed to observe and enjoy the perfume; if a narrow path system criss-crossing the bed is provided, innocent damage is reduced, although it can be argued that easy access will tempt someone to pick the flowers.

14.2. Reducing maintenance costs

A frequent directive in the brief for a landscape design is that the maintenance of the landscape should be minimal; the designer will certainly consider how the planting can be designed so that it will need very little attention. The reduction of repair and replacement of the planting is certainly one suggestion, but there are ways of reducing the conventional after-care operations by the provisions made in the design. As a first step, the retention of existing wild areas or the existing planting overcomes the initial extra maintenance operations, and a planting design for a wild area will lead to low maintenance, after some intensive weeding in the first year or two while the plants grow sufficiently to dominate (Plate 14). If it is feared that a wild area will look untidy, it can be given the appearance of a conscious design decision by having a well maintained edge, such as a mown grass strip.

The need for expensive pruning operations can be reduced by arranging the planting so that it does not interfere with buildings, foundations and services, as well as with the uses of the landscape. Generally, the work involved in pruning shrubs is likely to be less if the area is large because long and untidy branches have little visual significance when seen over a large area – in a natural landscape the untidiness may be the natural habit of the shrub, but again only acceptable in the large areas normally associated with natural landscapes. Similarly, the edging between grass and shrub areas can be less tidy over a long length than with a small shrub bed in a lawn. The grass under a group of several trees in parkland can be left uncut without appearing inappropriate, but with a single tree long grass around its base becomes more obvious. The inference in these comments is that large areas of planting do not look out of place if very little maintenance is carried out (Fig. 14.3).

A difficult decision in planting design is the spacing of shrubs in relation to achieving a mature appearance quickly and to maintenance costs. If shrubs are planted closely, say at 0.5 m centres with plants averaging 0.75 m in height ex-nursery, the gaps between them will close quickly, thus reducing weeding. But this spacing, for most shrubs, would inhibit their natural growth, lead to some losses through competition, and lose something of their characteristic habit through crowding. Thus, the designer has to make a decision whether to budget for a more intensive maintenance in the early

Fig. 14.3 A simple but effective garden landscape requiring very little maintenance.

years or to budget for a heavier first cost due to the greater number of plants and a less satisfactory visual result ultimately unless a percentage of plants are removed after a few years. Sometimes pressure is strong for a quick result, perhaps to give a developed appearance to a new housing estate. At other times, a compromise may be planned between the correct spacing for mature growth and reducing weeding in the early years; an average spacing of 1 m, with some closer and some wider spacings depending upon the species, is a workable figure. Some shrubs can be planted closely without inhibiting future growth, but these usually require a regular cutting back akin to the coppicing technique used with some trees for commercial purposes; the red stemmed dogwood is the shrub which comes readily to mind in this respect.

A design which includes hedges trimmed to the smooth surfaces and regular lines of walling will be expensive to maintain when realized, but some plants keep within reasonable bounds when used for hedging with little maintenance (Fig. 14.4). An example for a large hedge, both in height and length, is the Irish yew with its erect habit. Some hypericums, such as *Hypericum 'Hidcote'*, are compact plants and can make a tidy medium height hedge with little maintenance. The common box and its many varieties include plants that will form a miniature hedge, commonly known as edging, or a small hedge with comparatively little trimming or cutting.

The use of groundcover plants is frequently advocated as a maintenance saving device, avoiding regular attention, as with grass cutting, and with little

Fig. 14.4 A hedge of St. John's Wort which requires very little pruning or cutting.

158

or no weeding after establishment. Nevertheless, some groundcovers, like ivy, may overrun the area they were designed to cover and require periodic cutting back around the perimeter. Other groundcover plants, like heathers, become 'woody' in time and the area may need to be replanted unless young growth can be maintained by annually cutting back. An example of a frequently used groundcover plant which keeps to the planted area, with little maintenance once established, is *Hypericum calycinum*. When plants are used to form a textural or colour pattern, it is necessary to keep each species or variety within its pre-determined territory, which can be difficult because of the accessibility problem. If the design is such that the areas covered by the different plants abut one another, corrugated strips are marketed for pressing into the dividing line to keep the root systems from invading the adjoining territory. The example of the prairie type grassland with perennial flowering plants (see Section 10.1) is a special management problem which is best solved by retaining the services of an ecologist to watch and advise during the initial years after seeding. At the design stage, using grass seed mixtures comprising 'non-invasive' grasses such as some varieties of browntop (*Agrostis tenuis*), is likely to avoid excessive competition with the perennial flowering plants. There is also the possibility of reducing soil fertility (see Section 10.1) to restrict the growth of the grasses, leaving pockets of fertile soil at intervals into which perennial flowering plants will establish quickly and perhaps spread out into the less fertile surroundings.

14.3. Land uses and landscape management

Agricultural, afforestation and horticultural landscapes are self-maintaining through the commercial activity, but suggestions have been made for incorporating in amenity landscapes some of the uses associated with these rural industries. For example, large areas of parkland are used in the countryside for grazing, thus controlling the growth of the grass cover, and some examples are similarly managed in urban areas. Fruit-bearing trees and shrubs are examples of planting with a commercial value which can be set against their maintenance, but until society as a whole has a better social conscience with a consequent reduction of vandalism and stealing, and there is a greater determination and interest to design and organize landscape maintenance on a partial return basis, this suggestion is unlikely to be successful.

CHAPTER 15

Implementing the planting plan

It may be considered a naive observation to say that the contractor who carries out the planting must be provided with adequate information if the intentions of the designer are to be carried out accurately, but this does not always happen. Prior to the preparation of a working plan for carrying out the planting, the client will expect to be shown an indication of the appearance of his investment by means of sketch plans, perspective drawings, and sometimes by models of the proposals. A variety of techniques have been used to show planting (a selection is included in Fig. 15.1a–d), but it is difficult to give a full picture of planting proposals because of seasonal change, the many viewpoints, and the different appearance as the planting matures. Readers will, doubtless, be familiar with the Red Book technique of before and after views used by Humphrey Repton; for some projects it is possible to alter photographs of the existing landscape by overlaying the proposals using opaque colour.

15.1. Setting out

For use by the contractor, the information needs to be factual, rather than representational. Compared with working drawings of building and engineering construction, some landscape projects may not require the same degree of accuracy in the planting plans; for example, tree planting in groups on a large area of grassland may not interfere with the use of the area if the trees are planted 1 or 2 m away from the position planned by the designer, and it is doubtful whether he or anyone else would notice the difference. But, if the area has a tight arrangement of space for games, or a sight line at a road junction is a critical factor, accuracy is essential. Thus, the need for a dimensioned planting plan will depend upon circumstances.

Whether the planting plan is accurately dimensioned or not, a reference point or points is needed to relate the plan to the site, and this might be an existing building with a line extending one wall drawn across the plan. This line can be sighted and set out on the site, and from the line projections at right angles at suitable intervals are drawn on the plan and set out on site; where the lines cross or are near to planted areas, these latter can be scaled

Fig. 15.1 There are many drafting techniques for illustrating planting proposals on plan. The four techniques shown here are (a) a simple diagrammatic ink line technique, (b) an ink line technique which seeks to give a visual representation of the different plants, (c) a technique using tree stamps, and (d) drafting with a soft pencil, where the 'graining' of the pencil lines is sympathetic to the textural effect of the plants.

from the drawing and set out on site. If the site includes a building with a steel or concrete frame in course of erection, the sighting of opposite members of the frame from the site boundary will line up a series of parallel lines through the site and these are plotted on the plan, thus effecting a similar link between a reference point or line and the proposed planting (Fig. 15.2). Failing existing or new reference points, the planting can be set out by conventional chain survey methods.

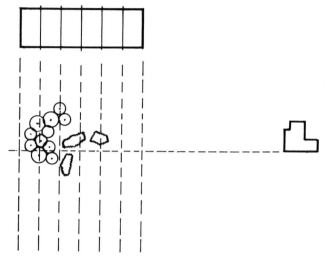

Fig. 15.2 Setting out the planting positions of trees and shrub groups by sighting along the walls or steelwork of buildings.

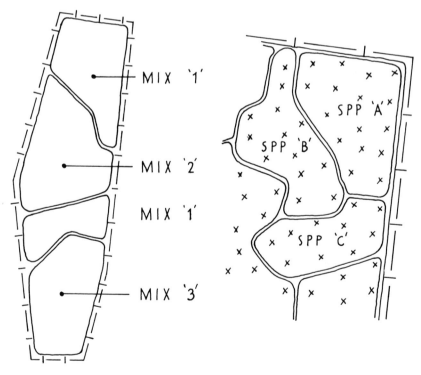

MIX '1'

MIX '2'

MIX '1'

MIX '3'

SPP 'A'

SPP 'B'

SPP 'C'

Fig. 15.3 On the left, a planting plan for a mixed woodland, and on the right, a detail to illustrate the arrangement of the species.

15.2. Planting detail

The scale and nature of the planting will influence the amount of detail on the planting plan. An area of mixed woodland can be satisfactorily planted from a plan which has a detail of a small part showing a typical arrangement of the different species (Fig. 15.3). On the other hand, a herbaceous border needs the position of every plant shown on the plan if the designer's intentions are to be fully realized. With the woodland, places can be marked to indicate where a greater percentage of one species is to be located for accentual effect.

15.3. Planting symbols

It is possible for a contractor to ascertain the number of plants of each species from a planting plan; reliance has to be placed upon his accuracy of measurement if the plan merely refers in a note to the spacing of the plants. The preparation of a list or schedule of plants by the designer or a quantity surveyor removes any element of doubt. The planting plan can be simplified by using numbers, letters or symbols referring to the list or schedule (Fig. 15.4); the numbers, letters or symbols should keep separate the different

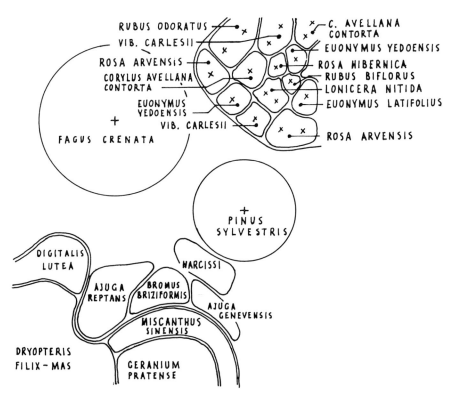

Fig. 15.4 A planting plan on which each plant is named and located, except the spacing of the perennials and groundcover plants would be described in the Key.

growth stages at planting time, thus, trees, shrubs, climbers, herbs, perennials, annuals, aquatics and semi-aquatics, divided as appropriate into bush, semi-mature, large, medium and small standards, whips, seedlings, groundcover plants, grass seeding and turfing. In the case of trees and shrubs, a further division under the headings deciduous, broad leaved evergreen, and coniferous is helpful, while the age or height of the plants at planting is necessary.

Some draftsmen use different symbols on the planting plan for the types of plant, but numbers or letters within a single tree or other plant symbol, and referring to the list or schedule, can give necessary information; for example, A.a.1.s where:

A to Z	= the type of plant, tree, shrub, climber, etc
a to z (extended as necessary to aa to zz)	= the species
1,2,3, etc	= height in metres above ground at planting
s	= seedling
w	= whip
ss	= small standard
ms	= medium standard
ts	= tall standard
sm	= semi mature
b	= bush tree
gc	= groundcover
r	= rooted perennial

An alternative method is to name the species by the side of the symbol, and if several plants of the same species are linked together with a line joining the centres of the symbols, the naming need only occur once. A plan drawn for the information of the client is helpful if the drafting technique differentiates between the types of plant.

A problem in drafting is the size of the span of a tree or shrub which should be shown on a planting plan. Ideally, there should be at least two versions, the first showing the span of the plants at the time of planting, and this is sufficient for the contractor. The second plan shows the forecasted span at maturity, with a broken line for those plants which should be removed after a certain period in order that the remaining plants can develop both vertically and horizontally in a more natural manner. It is possible to include all this information on one plan.

The drafting of beds containing shrubs, perennials, groundcovers etc. should indicate the perimeter of the bed clearly so that the contractor knows exactly where to change from grass or paving to the soil of the bed. While shrubs in beds are sometimes delineated by a symbol for each plant, they and the other types of plants in beds are often shown by a ring around the extremity of the vegetation of each species, and either name the species with

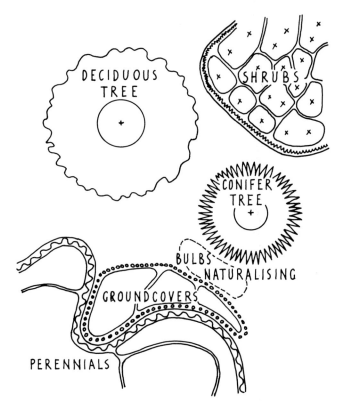

Fig. 15.5 A planting plan with a drafting technique which differentiates between the different kinds of plants.

the quantity, or use a reference as suggested previously with the quantity added. It is helpful to everyone if the drafting technique indicates the type of planting by an additional wavy or zigzag line around the bed (Fig. 15.5).

The scales often used for planting plans are shown below as a guide, but the scale used also depends upon the complexity of the information.

For woodland planting	1:500
For tree planting on sites up to public park size	1:200
For shrub, perennial and groundcover planting	1:100
For detailed planting, e.g. rock gardens	1:50

15.4. Specifying planting

The information on planting plans should be supplemented with a written description or specification of the quality of plants required, the source of supply, the methods of planting, and after care. The recommendations for these matters of the British Standards Institution are in the following publications[1]:

BS 4428	: 1969 with amendment AMD 938 of April 1972 – General Landscape Operations.
BS 3936	: Nursery Stock, Part I, Trees & Shrubs, Part 2, Roses, Part 4, Forest Trees, Part 5, Poplars and Willows for timber production.
BS 4043	: Transplanting semi-mature trees.

15.5. Contract procedure

The carrying out of planting should not be undertaken without a legally binding agreement with the contractor which sets out his responsibilities regarding the purchase of plants, the planting itself, and the nature and extent of his subsequent responsibility. The Form of Contract of the Landscape Institute requires that all materials are to be of the respective kinds and standards described in the Bill of Quantities, or Specification, and that any trees, shrubs or other plants which are found to be defective within the Defects Liability Period are to be replaced by the contractor at his own cost.

A question often asked concerns the source from which the plants are to be obtained. Particular nurseries can be specified, although it is wise to check first whether the plants are in stock; this procedure can lead to rather higher tenders because many contractors have nurseries with whom they deal at favourable rates. If the search for plants is left to the contractor, he should be required to obtain permission before ordering. Nurseries in similar climate and altitude conditions to those of the site are preferable sources of supply, but when this is not possible it is an advantage if arrangements can be made to buy in the plants a whole season prior to being required, and to plant them out temporarily in a nursery on the site so that some degree of acclimatization takes place. A site nursery is, in any case, sensible on a large project which cannot be planted within a short time.

It is a temptation to plant as early as possible on a site so that some growth occurs before completion of the project. Against this, however, should be set the risk of damage by other contractors on the site. Also, early planting exposes it to vandalism, the responsibility for which is difficult to determine when there is no 24 hour site supervision. If the specification requires the contractor to accept the responsibility for replacing vandalized plants, this is a dilemma for tendering contractors who have to guess at the cost of possible damage, and, if they place this too high, stand no chance of being successful. In any event, the client should be made aware of the problem and he may agree to a special contingency sum to be used as necessary for replacing vandalized plants.

A preliminary discussion with the contractor's foreman about planting methods and arrangements is advisable. This could include the suggestion that the planting drawings should be cut to convenient size and mounted on boards with a waterproof covering; also, the carrying out of a demonstration planting exercise so that there is no question about the meaning of the specification. Spot checks on the positions of the planting are advisable, but a completely comprehensive check of every position and the manner in which each plant is planted can only be carried out by a clerk of works, full time on the site.

The contractor's responsibilities during the Defects Liability Period should cover two seasons of growth, one being a full season and the other a sufficient time to check that growth has commenced again, with the Winter resting period between. Twelve months is the absolute minimum in this respect. The tasks that are likely to be found necessary in this period include keeping the plants well firmed in and securely tied to the stake in the case of standard trees, watering during dry spells in the growing season, and removing competition from weeds. If the contractor when estimating budgets for these tasks to result from several periods of dry and windy weather, his estimate is likely to be high. The employment by the client of his own maintenance staff as soon as all or part of the work is completed is theoretically an ideal situation, but the attitude often adopted when this happens is that the planting should be able to establish successfully under the planting procedure of the contractor without any maintenance, with an unsatisfactory conclusion for both the client and the contractor unless the work is handed over complete or in sections with a signed acceptance by the

Fig. 15.6 Gardeners preparing a bed of irises for the annual display in Japan.

Fig. 15.7 Although this method of maintaining a grass lawn in Spain is now regarded as impracticable because of the labour costs, it seems better related to the world of plants than the mechanical mower.

client. When the contractor is also the maintenance staff, as in a local authority parks department, this situation does not arise.

15.6. Maintaining the planting

The many tasks of, and materials needed for, maintaining the planting are well documented, with the exception that further research is needed into the prevention of wear and tear, and the keeping of ecologically based planting in a state not too far from the designer's intentions. It must be recognized, however, that planting is alive and has all the characteristics of growth, survival and death. Left to itself, without undue human influence, these characteristics find their place in a natural ecological system (Fig. 15.7). When the planting is not left to adjust to this system, but is to be kept in a different way decided by the designer, some degree of indefinite maintenance will be necessary (Fig. 15.6), and the instructions for it should be embodied in the planting design – a British Standard on landscape maintenance would complete the Standards already published on plants and planting.

References
[1] British Standards Institution, 2 Park Street, London W1A 2BS.

Appendix – Plant lists and further reading

Lists of plants suitable for various habitat conditions, such as shade, smoky atmosphere, wetlands and woodlands, and which give special effects like autumn colour and berries, can be found in Nursery catalogues and books on gardening; these are readily available. A plant list for British conditions is published by the Landscape Institute (12 Carlton House Terrace, London SW1Y 5AH) which is based on the experience of many persons in planting design.

In addition to these numerous sources, plant lists for special conditions are contained in the following books:

Kelway, C. (1970), *Gardening on the Coast*, David & Charles, Newton Abbot.

Wyman, D. (1956), *Ground Cover Plants*, Macmillan, New York.

Ingwersen, W. E. Th. (1951), *Wild Flowers in the Garden*, G. Bles, London.

Witham Fogg, H. G. (1974), *The Complete Handbook of Bulbs*, Ward Lock, London.

Grounds, R. (1974), *Ferns*, Pelham Books, London.

Perry, F. (1947), *Water Gardening*, Country Life, London.

Mansfield, T. C. (1942), *Alpines in Colour and Cultivation*, Collins, London.

Bean, W. J. (1946), *Wall Shrubs and Hardy Climbers*, Putnam, London.

Yarrow, A. E. (1973), Planting design and management for wildlife interest, *Landscape Design*, No. 102.

Caborn, J. M. (1965), *Shelterbelts and Windbreaks*, Faber & Faber, London.

Hackett, B. (1972), *Landscape Development of Steep Slopes*, Oriel Press, Newcastle-upon-Tyne.

Hackett, B. (ed.) (1971–2), *Landscape Reclamation*, Vols. I & II, I.P.C. Science & Technology Press, Guildford.

Mansfield, T. C. (1949), *Annuals in Colour and Cultivation*, Collins, London.

Mansfield, T. C. (1944), *The Border in Colour*, Collins, London.

Further reading

Birren, F. (1961), *Color, Form & Space*, Reinhold Publishing Corporation, New York.

Conder, J. (1893), *Landscape Gardening in Japan*, Dover Publications Inc., New York (republished 1964).

Hadfield, M. (1960), *Gardening in Britain*, Hutchinson, London.

Masson, G. (1961 & 1966), *Italian Gardens*, Thames & Hudson, London.

Miles, R. (1967), *Forestry in the English Landscape*, Faber & Faber, London.

Martineau, A. (1917), *The Herbaceous Garden*, William & Northgate, London.

Robinson, W. (1883), New edition, 1956. *The English Flower Garden*, (ed. Hay, R.), John Murray, London.

Index